What Top Athletes are Saying About Nick Gancitano *and* **THE EDGE OF GLORY**

"I knew Nick trained collegiate and NFL kickers, so I felt lucky to train with him. He spent countless hours refining the physical and mental aspects of my game and taught me awesome technical skills I use every day of my life! Nick constantly instilled in me that I can achieve anything. I worked hard, but none of my accomplishments would have been possible without the instruction, friendship and inspiration of Nick Gancitano."

—Blair Walsh, *Minnesota Vikings All-Pro Place-Kicker*

"This book offers a wealth of amazing insights, not just for athletes but for all. It quickly inspired profound transformations in my life and sport! Its message introduced me to an open-hearted way of living that changed my life. After reading Nick's first book, I got amped when I heard about this book for athletes, which felt like it addressed me directly. For every athlete on any level, *The Edge of Glory* is a must-read that will hone you into The Zone, so you can be at your best!"

—Scott Stewart, *Professional Wakeboarder*

"Whether you're new to martial arts or an accomplished veteran, this book is for you. *The Edge of Glory* is the perfect guide for directing you to your limitless potential!"

—Sensei Katherine Sanson, *Shio Karate Club*

"As a pro golfer, Nick's path into The Zone changed my life. I highly recommend *The Edge of Glory* to anyone who wants the absolute most out of their sport or career."

—Dennis Xiques, *Professional Golfer*

THE EDGE OF GLORY

THE ATHLETE'S INSIDE GUIDE TO GREATNESS

NICK GANCITANO

The ONE Press
Boca Raton, FL

Library of Congress Cataloging-in-Publication Data

The Edge of Glory: The Athlete's Inside Guide to Greatness
Nick Gancitano

p. cm.
ISBN: 978-0-9895018-3-5
Library of Congress Control Number: 2014942671
G14
10 9 8 7 6 5 4 3 2 1

Printed and Bound in the United States of America

Boca Raton, Florida
561.299.1150
www.TheOnePress.com

Dedication

To my loving wife and friend, Penelope.
I love you with all my heart.
Thank you for each
glorious moment.

Acknowledgments

THANK YOU to Penelope Love from the bottom of my heart for being my most intimate friend and wife to whom I am eternally grateful, and for the many other reasons I cannot possibly explain. Thank you for helping me recognize what this book truly represents, what it can become, and for helping me bring its information together for completion. Over the years, you have been such a precious comfort and nurturing influence, convincing me that this book needed to be shared with the masses to expose the divine in even the mundane. But most of all, I thank you for the affection, beauty, wisdom and strength that you constantly share with me.

Thank you to my late father, Nick Gancitano Sr., for an extraordinary childhood and the gentle, loving compassion, support, friendship and wisdom. One could not have a more beautiful parent as a model and mentor. What I learned about life, parenting and unconditional love from you is priceless and beyond words. Also, thank you for being the light that guided me through the most confusing years of life as a child, teenager and young man, ultimately laying the foundation for the happiness I experience continuously today.

Thank you to Blair Walsh for inspiring me to return to coaching with your passion and enthusiasm to be the best, and for the genius in you that brought out the best in me as a coach to articulate my coaching philosophy as the outline and eventual backbone of this book.

Thank you to Linda Gancitano, my sister, for inspiring me to play sports for the sheer joy of it and for being an extraordinary friend throughout life. I was and am blessed to have you in my life, as you are a picture of dedication and motivation for all you touch.

Thank you to the late Mark Heit for your inspiration and convincing me that I had what it takes to succeed. I remain grateful for the support you gave while I developed confidence as a soccer player and athlete, for which I now have complete faith in myself. This would ultimately help mold my passion for life as a young man and give me the courage to face any challenge on and off the field.

Thank you to the late Joe Paterno for teaching me that "you are never as good as you think you are when you're good, and you are never as bad as you think you are when you're bad." These profound words of wisdom helped me to never get down on myself for failure, and to never become egotistical with success.

—Nick Gancitano
Boca Raton, Florida, USA

Table of **CONTENTS**

INTRODUCTION

THE EDGE OF GLORY is a guide in every athlete's search for that miraculous *one moment in time,* which is not something found in the theoretical future, but now. When you revere the sacredness of what is always here, you recognize you are already in heaven, living as a glorious expression of the Infinite.

For this to make any sense, you must stop to really consider: what does *infinite* mean? What does it mean to say omnipresent, omnipotent and omniscient? It is a simple concept to grasp, because infinite means *all there is:* including everywhere, everything, every thought and every action. On the other hand, it is also beyond our capacity to totally comprehend the Infinite with a finite brain.

Why am I introducing this abstract concept into a book about how to achieve athletic greatness and ultimate success? Because you must first realize your infinite and eternal nature in order that you may attain the ultimate. Now, you may say that many extraordinary people throughout history have achieved their potential without contemplating the Infinite, yet I say: No. They have not! That is a fantasy. In fact, without knowing this in one's heart, a person does not even come close to realizing their destiny. Indeed, this depth of enlightenment is such a rare phenomenon that most usually have only a fleeting glimpse of this state of consciousness within their lifetime.

Now, we've all witnessed some athletes who demonstrate superior talent to others around them, allowing them to excel, but that is not the full breadth of success I'm speaking of here. The level to which I am referring surpasses mere mastery of the body—it is living in a glorious state of existence, where life becomes one continuous blessing after another.

There are few ways to understand this, given the world's agreed-upon beliefs, dogmas, constraints and incentives to conform, which lure many away from this realization. Still, there *is* a way to live in a constant state of heavenly joy where you see all things as yourself and you feel as though you are in a perpetual dance with the Divine: where every single occurrence—on and off the sports field—is known to be the supreme demonstration of life.

So my question for you is this:

If you learned there is a playbook for living on the edge of glory, for playing on the goal line between heaven and earth forever, would you want to know what it is?

"Sure, why not?" you might say. Yet be aware: it requires more than a lukewarm commitment to succeed in this game. It requires the ultimate devotion and perseverance. How so?

It is actually quite simple, though its two-fold application requires the utmost discipline. One, you must be devoted to truth. The truth being that you are actually the Infinite pretending to be finite—a nothing pretending to be something—the spiritual substance of all existence molding itself into physical matter through thought. And two, you must be willing to constantly practice feeling the presence of Self within. This is *The Zone*, wherein you are not only aware of your body, but the power of the Divine coursing through it. In this elevated state, you could say that you have a physical and nonphysical aspect to your being: the physical part of you, which performs action, and the nonphysical whole, which imagines and brings to your physical part whatever it wants to experience.

When Albert Einstein said, "Imagination is everything! It is a preview of life's coming attractions," he meant that all *physical* experiences are brought into *ex*-pression through the use of your *nonphysical* imagination. To fully understand this, you must remember: you are only temporarily a person, and you are not as distinctly "individual" as you may have been taught. In fact, you could say that you are to the Divine what a water droplet is to the ocean, where the ocean is everywhere and all divisions between its droplets are purely imaginary.

What is implied here? That everything is connected. You are actually everything, so you need not try to get better than you already are. All that is necessary is to *re-define yourself and hold that vision in your consciousness until your desire manifests.* For instance, when you say, "My three-point shot is terrible," this is the Infinite playing a game of limiting itself. It is the opposite of another thought you might have when you say, "I am awesome at hitting three-pointers." All that is needed is for you to ignore the first of these and repeatedly affirm the second, until it out-pictures in your world. This is the practical meaning of what Walt Disney meant when he said, "If you can dream it, you can achieve it."

One simple way to screen your thoughts is to treat every thought like a kick-ball pitch rolling in toward you. Either you reject it because it is not what you want...or you take it, you kick it. If undesirable, you throw it back to the pitcher and await a better pitch. In other words, you practice seeing thoughts coming to you in different ways until you like one—and then you repeatedly hold that thought as an image in your imagination until it condenses into your world.

THE DIVINE CREATES THROUGH YOU

Every desire you have and ask for is a demand to the universe from the Divine—expressing through you. *Whatever you hold in your imagination must be given to you*, simply because it is Existence wanting to create something. Thus, It uses a physical body to do so—your body.

As such, *The Edge of Glory* affirms the perfection of your desires and supports you with focusing the energy of desire into a point of intention, so you may see your dreams come true.

TAKE IT TO THE LIMIT, LITERALLY

Perhaps you've been taught you should strive to be unlimited, to not want any limitations—but oh yes, you do! If you did not, you'd be shooting the ball in every direction simultaneously. Think about it: without limitations, you'd be doing everything at once and things would get mighty confusing. Deliberately restricting yourself through creative imagination is how you mold your world. It is customizing your "limitations of choice" through mental imagery.

The key to consciously fulfilling your dreams is the deliberate selection of your realities *in your imagination first*. Understand, you are both the Dreamer of this dream, and also the dream itself. You are all of it and you are entitled to have your dreams come true.

As a former athlete, and a coach for more than twenty-five years, I have written this book to help point out some unconscious limitations reportedly arising in athlete's minds. Once you have pinpointed these self-defeating thoughts, you can then uproot them and rearrange your mind, thereby projecting a new world that gives full expression to your divine purpose as a player... not only on your sports team, but also in your life.

HOW TO USE THIS BOOK: PRACTICING YOUR AFFIRMATIONS

The "active ingredient" of this book is its prescribed affirmations for those desiring the ultimate fulfillment of their destiny. Whenever you utilize these powerful affirmations—specialized spoken commands—you are physically demonstrating the unlimited potential of the Divine within you. You have been blessed, ordained even, with the capacity of speech, making you capable of creating through the spoken word, which magnetizes *whatever* you ask for!

The Edge of Glory affirmations are particularly effective when written or spoken aloud *and felt*, since this potent combination accelerates the process of bringing thoughts from the mental plane into your physical reality.

AN IMPORTANT NOTE ON INCORPORATING MUSIC INTO YOUR AFFIRMATION PRACTICE

Since the subconscious mind is far more easily impressed through sound, you may wish to incorporate inspirational music into your daily affirmation practice by allowing it to play in the background. Because all things correspond with a particular frequency, every note and lyric in a song is creative and shapes your reality. Take, for instance, the words in the Billy Joel song, "Pressure." What could be the value in a song with lyrics that add pressure to your life by speaking the word? Know that some music has a potent higher vibrational quality, which liberates you by making heavenly things seem more easily attainable. For example, I have yet to meet a person who is not inspired by Whitney Houston's "One Moment in Time." There is a reason it was selected as the theme song for the 1988 Olympic Games. So, be selective and choose your music wisely!

Combining your spoken word with harmonic music launches your affirmations forward with tremendous creative power, so use all these to your advantage. I recommend you sit with your selection of affirmations in a place where you will not be distracted, so you can experience more rapid results. This said, I invite you to adopt the understanding:

> *If this heavenly vision that I dream of*
> *is truly my destiny, then try as I may,*
> *I cannot lose it. And if it is not*
> *of the Divine, then give me an*
> *equivalent result...or greater.*

As you apply this wisdom to your game and your life, please feel free to communicate your experience, recommend elite athlete video links and share insights with me and other *Edge of Glory* readers. I wish you a blessed journey playing the game that only you were meant to play while living on the edge of glory.

—Nick Gancitano

Chapter

1

MASTER THE BASICS

Few things are as important as mastering the basics in life. In the sports world, one has only to consider how many different pitches an MLB pitcher needs to perfect in his repertoire. Three, maybe four? And how many swings does a golfer need to win the PGA? Or different strides for a horse to win the Triple Crown? The answer...not many. In fact, you can count them on one hand. Then, the key becomes how consistently you can perform these few motions, pitches, swings or strides. Your consistency gives an opposing coach fits because they cannot defend against refined skill, ergo: one must Master The Basics!

There is not much more to say about training except, keep it simple.

This does not mean you abandon your playbook or game plan; it means that all drills should reinforce basic skills so they become second nature.

Once the basics become natural, more complex skills can be sprinkled in, though I generally don't find them necessary. In all my years of experience, I've never seen a complicated system beat a simple one with sound skill development, all other variables being similar. The more complex your system, the greater the difficulty involved with getting players familiar with their teammates' habits and patterns. It doesn't really matter if the other team knows your habits, so long as you can do more than one thing well. The reason for this is during the course of gameplay the opponent will have to guess how to defend you and thinking takes time—time to react, time they won't have during the game.

Some will argue that *sophisticated* is offsetting, because the other team will find it difficult to defend...but they won't. Not if they're well prepared. An experienced coach is not overly concerned unless the opposing team has blistering speed. Therefore, the key is not in trickery, but in faith, momentum, sound basic skills, speed and conditioning, in that order. Hence, the more fearless you are—while able to control field position and possess the ball offensively—the greater your chances of winning a championship.

What about the good old double reverse? Does it look good? Sure—if it works. But it usually doesn't.

Once in a while perhaps, but the colleges and professional offenses don't repeatedly run dives, veers and sweeps because they statistically fail. All coaches know that simple works unless you're just too obvious.

A team that relies on trickery is trying to compensate for their lack of personnel or preparation. Do your homework, so that you don't need to get fancy. Be strong, fast, unpredictable—and master the basics.

Affirmation

I am a master of the basics.

NOTHING ASSURES SUCCESS LIKE YOUR ENJOYMENT

THE SHEER JOY OF PLAYING is always sufficient. It makes any experience worthwhile. There is no need to attach undue pressure to yourself to achieve what can never be known in advance anyway, namely—the final outcome. What is the point? Can you remove one ounce of stress by thinking about winning while you're playing? This is like trying to play basketball, wearing old, stretched-out shorts and using one hand to hold them up while playing with only the other. It is simply an unnecessary burden. Likewise, why bother playing if you're not going to relax and enjoy?

One of the greatest problems facing dominant teams on any level is the self-imposed pressure to win at the price of losing their love of the game. For decades, I've coached sports and I have discovered that the team or players having the most fun always play the best.

In fact, I have yet to notice an unhappy athlete who performs optimally. Perhaps they are skilled, but they are not remotely close to being in *The Zone*. It can even be said that one enters the door to *The Zone* only through what they enjoy or feels good to them—and from there, success is inevitable.

My attitude is if you always do what you enjoy, then you are in alignment with the divine plan and you will be blessed with success. So always have fun before the game and carry it in with you!

Affirmation

My life is one continuous blessing after another, so I succeed effortlessly while doing precisely what I enjoy most.

THE TARGET NEVER MOVES IF YOUR MIND IS STILL

THERE IS AN ASTOUNDING phenomenon that occurs while practicing in a meditative state: what most people refer to as *The Zone*. To be in *The Zone* means that your mind is still—there is pure experience without thought. From there, whatever target you're focused on will hold steady and not budge.

This precise clarity provides the sense that you are everywhere—that in this moment, you are the entire ocean of existence. Then, there is no chance of failure, because who would fail if you are the whole reality?

Over the years, I have acquired special exercises to deepen the stillness that leads to this realization. These powerful relaxation techniques minimize mental chatter; and with practice, they can eliminate all unnecessary thoughts and consequently, all suffering. Because without thought, how can there be suffering? Suffering is only a thought, yet beyond thought, there is bliss...true spiritual ecstasy.

Once you have tasted this bliss, you will do virtually anything necessary to acquire it again. You will become engrossed with attaining what the prophets and sages throughout history have spoken of. And it does not have to stop when you leave your athletic practice; it can stay with you always. In fact, it is always here within you. In truth, it is You—Your True Self.

There is an experiment you can do to prove this to yourself conclusively. The relaxation sequence takes only twenty to thirty minutes. As an owner of this book, you may obtain your audio download of the exercise at www.NickGancitano.com. Most people prefer using this audio version until they re-member the sequence and can do it independently.

Once you can still your mind on the spot, you'll be aware of your Self as the entire space and field, the sky—everything. Then, when you strike or shoot the ball, there will no longer be thoughts or doubts about success. Each movement will be total and perfect.

Affirmation

*I live in a perpetual state of peaceful contentment,
fulfilling all my intentions with miraculous ease.*

GOT EXPECTATIONS?

ALL EXPECTATIONS ARE a guaranteed limitation. Now, this flies in the face of what almost everyone has been taught: that you must expect to do well, that you must demand perfection. But this is not the truth because expectation kills passion.

Perhaps you have a personal goal of scoring a single touchdown or goal every game. This becomes a problem, because you possibly could have scored three each game if you had not been intent on scoring just one. After one score, you've let up because you reached your quota for the day and decided to coast through the rest of the game...not consciously, yet it is there, programmed into your subconscious. Thus, the expectation has become the limitation.

Expectations also create tension. Consider the feeling when someone expects you to do something. There is a need for you to succeed—an obligation. This is the opposite of freedom, because the last thing you want to think about is how well you are doing, or what you are not doing. It should be enough that you are enjoying yourself. There should be no demands on you, no concerns about the outcome. The result is determined in the passion of play, by your love of the game—not by thinking about it.

Now, I am not saying that you shouldn't have any intentions, as with fulfilling an objective, no. I say no expectations so you become watchful of the more subtle, invisible weight that anchors you in obligation to being what others want you to be, oftentimes without your even knowing it.

Perhaps you've won fifteen or twenty games in a row and the pressure to break the record draws near. And so the media's countdown begins. Where instead of just enjoying the game, you get caught up in the news hoopla: it can happen to the best of the best. In fact, it is usually happening to them the most since they are generally the most visible. Because when athletes, teams or even companies are on the verge of greatness, there is often an unspoken fear that is avoided—the fear of success. And the fear of success is just the flip side of one's fear of failure.

With celebrities, there is a sort of moral expectation placed on them to be role models for children and others. Being exalted as a role model exacerbates the stress because you have pretended to not notice it. Or more dangerous, you may assert that you don't care and take the posture of indifference. Either way, the tendency is to downplay it in your mind, thinking, "I'm above this childishness." Or "I'm a professional," so you strive to act like a pro—whatever that is supposed to look like. You pretend, "If I don't talk about it, it will miraculously disappear." No. Because with this approach, whether you never discuss it or you are constantly talking about it, it has utterly saturated your mind. Either extreme is the problem: thinking outwardly or thinking inwardly to yourself. So it is better to bring it up, and keep things in perspective by being aware. By being conscious of these potential traps, you eventually become wise in the ways of media politics.

And should you find yourself in a position of great expectations, watch your thoughts and fears. If you observe them within your mind, they will disappear; if you ignore them, they will follow you. When going into battle, it is always better to know where the enemy's land mines are located. Do not pretend to know so you look brave. At any threshold, "Wisdom is the better part of valor."

With the recognition of fear, there is grace, because fears are only dangerous when undetected. Avoid fear however, and the fear becomes powerful, more destructive: like a bomber squadron that has penetrated by flying below your radar screen. Yet, if you shine your awareness on fear, it must leave, like a bomber that has been detected on its approach— it must flee because it is now being watched.

Finally, expectations tempt one to compromise, so don't lie to yourself about what you want, or you eventually come to resent others because you didn't speak or live your truth. What could be the benefit of compromising? This is precisely what happens when one is overwhelmed by fame: they become unable to fulfill the immeasurable demands placed on them. On the outside, yes—you'll be very calm and poised, yet if you are not conscious, the tension of feeling obligated will creep in and sabotage your dreams.

Champions are never afraid to confront the enemy, even if it is in their own mind. Awareness of hidden obligations to satisfy other people's expectations disarms the saboteur so you can fulfill your ultimate potential.

Affirmation

I always want what I always get, so I always get what I always want.

HOW YOU FEEL BEFORE THE GAME USUALLY DETERMINES HOW YOU FEEL AFTER IT

MOST PEOPLE LIVE under the impression that they can only be happy if they get what they want, so they agonize during the period preceding it. Unfortunately, that's just not the way life works. Because how you feel about something beforehand is precisely what draws it to you and makes it real. So if you're waiting impatiently, feeling anxious and damning the seconds for loitering, you will only draw to you more anxious waiting. Why not pretend you already have what you want?

Ask yourself, "How would it feel right now if I already won my match?" That's right: you should fake it until you make it.

My good friend, Kevin Kopka, was a place-kicker in high school, and capable of hitting field goals from about 60 yards pretty consistently. Still, he insisted that he could hit from 70 yards, even though as his coach I had never seen it happen. At the time, 60 yarders were somewhat of an anomaly, but 70 yarders were unheard of. I didn't say anything, somewhat puzzled by this colossal exaggeration. Yet I became concerned when it leaked out to a major newspaper in the area—I had the thought that this was going to blow up in his face.

Just as I suspected might happen, a reporter had scheduled to attend one of the football practices to see the white elephant perform—to see him kick a 70-yard field goal. Well, he didn't make a 70 yarder, but he did manage to kick two successive 71 yarders, yes—back to back! And though I was his coach, he taught me more in that one day than I taught him in all the years I coached him.

So don't ever agree with people's beliefs or concepts about anything until you experience them for yourself. *It does not matter what others think about you unless you agree with them.* Then only will their limitations become yours—only if you believe them.

You must feel it in your heart first—then the outcome or physical expression is merely the confirmation of what you already know to be true. Remember, your job is to act like that which you want to be, thereby demonstrating perfect faith that you are already what you desire.

Affirmation

*I am joyously immersed in this glorious life,
realizing my unlimited potential.*

THE MORE YOU EXPERIENCE, THE LESS YOU FEAR

BEING A COACH AND TEACHER for decades, I've encountered many techniques and processes designed to help people transcend fear. And the basic stumbling block I've discovered with these techniques is that when someone applies them, it is usually with the intention of getting rid of fear rather than investigating more deeply what fear actually is—or more importantly, who is afraid?

Let me first say: all attempts to remove fear are futile. Whatever you resist will persist, because any attempt to destroy fear is rooted deeply in the actual *fear of fear itself.*

For this reason, I am therefore proposing a powerful, non-resistance method to help you rise above even the fear of fear itself.

It is simple: experience fear outright! Be willing to look at fear, in fact, notice every facet of life. Not only the pleasant things either, because how can you enjoy life without tasting the sweet and sour? By experiencing fear, you realize there is nothing to be afraid of—you find that everywhere you look, there is beauty. Instead, many people run from fear and allow their illusions to dominate their lives.

I once heard a story: a man dies and as he is approaching the Pearly Gates, he is greeted by Saint Peter, who asks him, "Where are your scars?" The man says, "I have none." So Peter asks, "Was there nothing worth dying for? Nothing worth living for?"

Clearly, such a man lives in fear, constantly playing it safe and never taking chances. The reason fear is such a strange phenomenon is that it is not actually real, yet it discourages us from doing the things we enjoy most.

Consider yourself walking home in the dark at night as a child: how every sound and shadow seemed like a horror movie. Remember how you'd allow your imagination to run wild: the shadows of the tree branches behind you, cast ahead by the streetlight, created a monster projected onto the street before you. Yet, upon turning to face the creature, as it gained on you, it was revealed to be a tree limb and you felt instantly relieved. Nothing was eliminated; all that was necessary was to face the truth. This is how your fears have managed to survive—in the shadows. Yet, when your fears are confronted, they disappear; because once you've experienced something, you no longer fear it.

One common fear many athletes encounter is that of facing a larger opponent. I remember watching Olympic wrestling as a boy. The American was a 436 pounder named Chris Taylor, and he was facing the German, Wilfried Dietrich. Dietrich was much smaller, maybe half Taylor's weight, if that. I remember being shocked at the immensity of Taylor, whom I had never seen before. "How could they be in the same weight class?" I wondered. It seemed impossible; Taylor was enormous! Yet, somehow, it happened: Dietrich got his arms around Taylor and executed a full frontal suplex—and pinned him. From that point forward, I never feared larger opponents again. It was truly a miraculous healing, because I then realized that size was irrelevant amidst other factors. A must-see on YouTube: http://www.youtube.com/watch?v=n79wBw_LJ9Y

Having a revelation based on observation can certainly trigger insight and release one's fears. *Yet the surefire means of transcending fear is to find out,* *"who am I that is afraid?"*—which is like turning the lights on in a dark room, where all is safe again. Nothing is added or removed. Simply turn inward and poof, the reality is revealed. In the light of awareness, we find that most things we feared were not even there in the first place, and we are free.

Affirmation

I fearlessly embrace all experiences, knowing each situation is a perfect opportunity for me to realize who I am.

ALL GENIUS ARISES FROM LISTENING TO THE INNER COACH

THERE COMES A TIME in everyone's life when they must remove their coaches, parents and preachers from the pedestal—the power hierarchy must be destroyed. If not done so consciously, you will never develop a champion's confidence. The playing field must be leveled. A friendship must replace the teacher-student relationship. Once this takes place, one's true genius arises.

The inner voice, the coach within, takes over and the outer coach becomes a faded memory. A lifetime with the same coach or teacher is not necessary. Where you once were in awe of them, they will now sound redundant. Your life has become your coach; the creator of the world has become your teacher. Allow this insight to illuminate your vision. It does not mean to reject anyone—no, because if you and your coaches can accept each other as equals, a friendship can emerge. The split can be seamless, even a celebration, because they will honor your evolution into independence. If they are not blinded by ego, they will recognize you no longer need them. If not, if they attempt to keep you as their student, then a break from them is necessary. It may be temporary, who can say? An enlightened coach understands this essential need for equality and freedom. If they do not, then the split is just as necessary for them as it is for you.

At the very least, you must understand the rights to your freedom, because nobody can tell you what to do with your life. No, not even your parents. If you do not establish independence, you will remain in their shadow, when you could quite easily step into the light.

How exactly does one transcend the need for the outer coach to discover the inner one? What is this inner coach? It is your inner voice—the divine voice of wisdom that only you can know as it pertains to your life. Not the egoic selfish voice in the head, but your inner knowing. It is your intuitive guidance that comforts you when you humbly listen. In its wake, there is a deep sense of peace and relaxation, a flow of comforting stillness. It will not sound repressive or authoritative, but inspirational.

Be still and feel the Divine within you...
in the depths of your own consciousness. Close
your eyes and feel "I am." From there, all life's
answers will flow to you from a spring of previously
untapped wisdom. You will be filled by the power
of it and know the Truth. Then only will the genius
within you be released.

Affirmation

I now open the floodgate for the divine plan of my life to manifest, allowing the genius within me to now be expressed.

Chapter

8

DO NOT CHANGE YOUR GAME PLAN OR YOU WILL LOSE

NEARLY EVERY PROBLEM people face in life revolves around the attempt to satisfy others. This also means, of course, that you then expect others to satisfy you by giving you what you want or becoming what you want them to be. The problem, oddly enough, has nothing to do with satisfying others, but the very idea of "other." When one focuses on "other," they forget themselves.

Eleven players gathered in a locker room preparing for their game. As they started counting themselves to make sure all had arrived, they noticed that they were one player short. As game time approached, each one counted, but still found only ten and so they became very worried. At that moment, the coach asked them to sit down so he could go over the starting lineup. As he noticed their anxious faces, he asked them what was wrong. They told him one player was missing. The coach then had them sit in a line and with his hand, he touched each of them on the shoulder as he counted down the line. Upon touching the eleventh man, he declared that all eleven were accounted for. Realizing that each player had forgotten to include himself, they became very relieved to find they were all present.

People forget themselves and get caught up in the world and its apparent problems—so they suffer. Likewise, in athletics, when you worry about what your opponent is doing, you forget to focus on what you yourself are doing, and in the process, you forget your objective: to play your game. If you do not recognize this preoccupation with your opponent, you miss the subtle fact that deep within you, you are thinking, "I have to stop them," rather than, "they need to stop us." This subtle shift of trying to stop "them" puts you on your heels, desperately back-peddling, afraid and defending, instead of on your toes— playing your game and creating opportunities.

This often happens when coaches feel they must win to preserve their jobs, or if you're playing to win a championship. The evidence of this will be clear by one's playing to "not lose," which is suicide. Just because you're on defense, this does not mean that your opponent is a threat to you; because you are not actually playing the man, but a role or position. There is an enormous difference when you approach a game this way: you do not get too lost in emotions regarding an unfavorable situation, and you can stick to your original game plan without overreacting.

"The best defense is still a good offense." When you're offensive, you are usually too focused on playing to worry about the other team. Instead, the players become like mannequins, positioned on the field only for you to practice scoring. *To remain in The Zone, don't adjust anything!*

If you are in the flow, there is no contest. The key here is to keep your pace high, and when you are playing your game, your presence is felt by the other team, even if you are not physically touching them. They will sense it in the air, in the space. If you are confident in your ability, you do not need to change your game. However, it is important to possess true confidence and not merely fake it, because you cannot pretend to be superior to an opponent that has prepared better; you must know— or at least, temporarily believe—you are better. You can convince your teammates of this. There is an art to this approach, so be creative. Develop the attitude that your opponents must stop you, not the other way around. This does not mean you ignore the other team's talent; rather, you formulate a comprehensive strategy to exploit your opponent's weaknesses, and then play your game: *the game that got you to the championship in the first place.*

Affirmation

I give thanks for this perfect life where miracle follows miracle in a continuous flood of success that never ends.

Chapter

9

CHAMPIONS ALWAYS FIND EACH OTHER

I HAVE OFTEN WITNESSED the same physical problems occurring with athletes from completely unrelated sports. For instance, many with knee injuries possess an impatient attitude of do or die. "Either I do it now, or it is over for me and someone will replace me!" Of course, this is foolish. Why would an athlete aim such a destructive thought at their future?

And since fear leads to stress, they have become tense and are no longer having fun. It almost seems some are more interested in worrying about the future or trying to prove something to the world instead of just playing the game.

It is common in competitive societies for people to contend for their resources. Many even acquire a

35

survival-of-the-fittest attitude, believing that if others have something, then they cannot also have it. Hence, they want others to fail, so they can acquire it and be in sole possession of *it*.

Yet nothing could be further from the truth! When you want others to succeed, you reach to yet greater heights, because your wanting others to be fulfilled carries a vibrational quality similar to your own happiness.

When feeling happy for others or loving them, we retain that same vibration in our own consciousness, which elevates our thoughts to that level, attracting the same types of experiences to us. For instance, it is far more common for scouts to flock to a multitude of great athletes, dramatically increasing the probability of being discovered or recruited at that location.

It is a fact: *winners attract winners!* This can't be refuted. Excellence has an irresistible feeling, drawing similar talent together, because like energies attract like. This is why some programs generate championship teams year after year. And though it may be possible to develop champions from an expansion program, it generally occurs with a mature program and a seasoned coach who understands how to inspire players and fans to *know* they will win. Even some of the more successful multilevel marketing companies, such as A. L. Williams—founded by a football coach, Art Williams—owe their success to unselfishness and the attitude of "Pushing Up People."

So, what about your opponents? Should you want them to be successful when you are striving for the same championship title? This may surprise you, but...yes! Not that you want them to beat you, yet you still want them to be at their best, because it raises the caliber of talent on the field, where everyone plays to a higher level of ability and enjoyment. Sure, winning and losing are a factor on some level, but they are not the primary focus in success. Inspiration, enthusiasm and enjoyment are. These three constitute the emotional playing field where champions find each other, congregate and develop into world-class athletes.

Affirmation

Through grace, success comes to me effortlessly as I relax and just have fun.

Chapter

PLAY AND LIVE LIKE A CHAMPION, OR SIT IN THE BLEACHERS

ATHLETICS ARE AN AREA IN LIFE where if you are not fully invested, then what is the point of playing at all? This may sound harsh, yet for each of us there is the perfect self-expression. If one is not committed to finding it, they become lost and parasitic. To invest totally means putting less essential matters on the back burner and focusing on what feels good and true to us, allowing us to transcend feelings of stagnation and apathy. A champion knows what this means on and off the field, so why not do the very best you can in every situation?

It is ideal to give your complete and undivided attention to one thing at a time. Yet, in today's world, with the advent of tablets, smartphones and other entertainment media, it almost seems many are intentionally being less productive and also less present. Some people even drive while texting. Will texting while playing sports be next?

Multitasking is a disturbance to being mentally cognizant in life. Those who do essentially guarantee they will not reach their full potential. *The object of the game of life is to effectively still your mind, where you can see clearly and eliminate incoherent mental pictures of confusion and uncertainty, replacing them with clear mental pictures of success.*

When your attention is divided, your mental energy is dissipated and weak, preventing you from focusing. This stops you from recognizing what is necessary to fulfill your purpose.

According to the Kaiser Foundation, in 2010, eight to eighteen-years-old devoted an average of 7 hours and 38 minutes to using entertainment media per day; that's over 53 hours a week or 2,756 hours per year. And, again, that was in 2010! What would your life be like if you spent that same time playing a sport, practicing a musical instrument or picturing those things in life you would like to have? Even if you are completely inexperienced in a particular area, with that amount of time properly channeled, you could become highly competent and accomplished. You could be a virtual phenom in whatever area you want to succeed. You must decide: what is more important to you? Then focus there.

Affirmation

I now open the way for my perfect expression, allowing my divine right to now reach me in tidal waves of success.

DON'T DO IT—BE IT!

IT IS RARE TO FIND THOSE who fully actualize their dreams. Perhaps you have had glimpses of extraordinary accomplishments. You recognize it upon witnessing such awe-inspiring beings, because you are left speechless. A thrill arises from deep inside you. A fortuitous flow of creativity surges through you: the feeling of such inspiration, you must go out and play at halftime. It's contagious!

Why is it such an anomaly to come across such athletes, when within each of us is a wellspring of divine grace? What prevents it, this cup that runneth over? In a word: *doing.* By "*doing,*" I mean trying to direct the flow of the stream, fighting against the natural current of life. So stop it! Trust life.

The river of life is flowing, yet conditioned into most people's minds is the belief that you must, "by the sweat of your brow," paddle against the current even when life is already happening on its own.

"Sitting and watching, spring comes and the grass grows all by itself." What does this mean? It means that the Source of all existence does not need help running the universe: It is already doing so. In fact, It effortlessly accomplishes everything while simultaneously "doing" nothing whatsoever. When we understand this, we take a giant leap toward recognizing the awesome power of the Supreme Being within. Not that you can ever understand It, but you can let go into the divine stream of life when you are witness to it and be humbled by Its Power.

Affirmation

Free from the burden of individual doing, I surrender and allow life to prosper through me.

ONLY INNER DISCIPLINE BRINGS SUCCESS

DISCIPLINE IS PERHAPS one of the most misunderstood words in the English language. Because of its root word "disciple," many have come to believe it suggests another person is higher than you, or administering some form of punishment upon you for misbehaving. A second idea relates to a disciplined struggle to attain a goal through a regimen of austerities, under which people must assert intense effort to overcome inherent flaws in their nature and accomplish a grandiose achievement.

Neither of these represents the true spirit of discipline, which has nothing to do with anyone else *but you.* Because true discipline is nothing other than your intuition urging you on in pursuit of your supreme destiny. Therefore, to whom should you listen to but your own inner guidance system if you truly aspire to freedom and your highest self-expression?

On the deepest and most sublime level, the Real You is like a droplet that has lost its boundaries in the ocean of Existence. True discipline is not a punishment. It cannot be imposed upon you by someone else. It must be directed through divine inspiration. If it is not, then it is not true discipline.

To achieve success through discipline, there must be inspiration minus any sense of obligation. Only then can you rise to success on the higher levels of athletics.

Affirmation

I am grateful for my perpetual state of happiness and the inner guidance and inspiration that allows for success to be drawn to me effortlessly.

Chapter

THOSE OBSESSED WITH WINNING WILL CHEAT

Perhaps you can recall a family member or friend who cheats when you play board games or sports. You know what I'm talking about: they're the one who is usually talking loudest in the crowd or doing outrageous things to get attention.

If it is you, don't worry—the omniscient One doesn't make mistakes. The proof of this is that before you were even born, when you were still in your mother's womb, the entire world was preparing for you.

Parties were planned, clothing was received, gifts were offered and a bedroom was prepared. A name was even assigned to you in preparation of your much anticipated arrival on the scene. At this point, your body was nothing but a clump of cells floating in water. Still, the Infinite One prepared the way for you. You did nothing, nor do you ever need to do anything to deserve the bounty of your inexhaustible supply. Uncertain of this, most societies on Earth have convinced people that bigger, better, faster and smarter is the way to happiness. Many have even been convinced that if they become those things and stand out from the crowd, then they will be happy—this is not always true.

If you recall those moments in life when you are the happiest, you are usually waking up from sleep and haven't had the slightest thought about anything yet. Or, perhaps you were walking in nature or on a beach holding hands with someone dear to you. The obsession with winning or being the best is nowhere to be found in such moments. In fact, the need to win is not a priority for those who are *truly* successful, but it is for those who are not yet there.

Do you disagree? Most people do—at first. Then I ask them, "How do you define success?" My simple definition for success is: the ability to be happy.

Under this definition, I find few who have found true and lasting success because most are concerned with the *quantities* in life rather than *quality*.

As such, most are so obsessed with being the best—or more importantly, better than others— that they will do virtually anything for the title of "winner," including give up their happiness. They will even cheat, which seems strikingly odd given that if you do win under such circumstances, you would know that you really lost. So what is the point? To know you've lost, but have others think you won? Cheating is the lazy and foolish man's path to success, a façade that embraces a false ideal: "It really does not matter if I enjoy life, so long as others admire me." And those cheaters atop the power pyramid must endure loneliness because false success often makes them intimidating to others. No one feels safe around them and there is a feeling deep down that this person is lying to me.

Unaware of others' motives, it becomes difficult to open the gates of authentic friendship and intimate relationships for such people. So being on top dishonestly has its price. This is what makes one who cheats so miserable.

If you win dishonorably, you have a false victory that cannot offset your loneliness and suffering. Understand, when you win, you are only there on top for a flicker. And if you are at the top less than honorably, it is impossible to stay there by honorable means so your entire life becomes a lie to sustain your pole position. This is why so many scratch and claw their way to the top to taste the glory, but it slips between their fingers. And just how often can one cheat their way to victory without being exposed? Aside from this, they have missed the glory, because happiness doesn't come from winning.

If winning were the source of happiness, then the biggest, best, fastest, strongest and richest in the world would be the happiest, when they clearly are not.

Balance, harmonious teamwork, love, friendship, service to others and integrity are the pillars of a lasting foundation rooted in happiness. Please do not believe me on this—look for yourself.

Affirmation

My life is a divine harmony of perfect integrity.

BALANCE ALWAYS WINS CHAMPIONSHIPS!

PERHAPS THE MOST COMMON reason for failure is the underdevelopment of life skills that transform beginner athletes into seasoned ones: I call it balance. Without balance, a team or individual cannot win a championship. It is also extremely rare to win a championship with only young, strong, inexperienced talent; it requires the addition of a balanced combination of seasoned players along with young eyes and fresh legs.

An example of an unbalanced athlete is a golfer with a tremendous driving shot who cannot win big tournaments because his/her middle and short game is not up to par. Strength, endurance, flexibility, awareness, agility and strategic comprehension must all crescendo simultaneously. The physical and mental must also come together with the individuals for a team to be in harmony and ready for a run at a championship.

The ultimate occurs when not only individual athletes and the team come into balance, but also its coaches, trainers, and if very fortunate, the players' families and fans. This is why teams that can rally an entire town or nation behind them fare well year after year.

Remember, all things considered equal, the balanced player or team will win. Balance provides adaptability: the ability to change and adjust to unpredictable circumstances as they arise. And, one thing is certain—they always arise.

Affirmation

Having totally surrendered and come into balance, my work is done so my heart's desires manifest.

DON'T GIVE INTERVIEWS OR WATCH THE NEWS

WHAT IS THE POINT of giving interviews about yourself? Give all the glory away and let the Infinite intelligence handle your publicity.

There is a law of prosperity, a spiritual law: "Whatever you give away, comes back to you multiplied." Also, let us be honest: if you must sing to the beat of your own drum, then you are only temporary—old news by suppertime or a tweet about to fall off the Twitter feed. There is no need to boast about yourself, because if you have to, then others are not.

Humility prepares you to deal with the media. If you are news-worthy, I have found that it is usually not wise to offer the media anything beyond, "Thank you for recognizing my efforts to play notably at the level I currently am."

Realize that no player is an island in the sports world, even those playing a more individualistic sport. Share the light with your teammates, coaches, parents and anyone who has contributed, because it takes nothing away from you and puts things in perspective—that nobody does it alone.

For this, I must coin my college football coach Joe Paterno, the winningest football coach in collegiate history. He told us to be very clear with what we said to the media, because they often spin words unfavorably. In fact, he often recommended that we *not* read what the newspapers were saying about us because as he put it, "You're never as good as you think you are when you're good, and you're never as bad as you think you are when you're bad."

Affirmation

My tongue yields so I need not speak of myself or others, as I simply abide in Self awareness.

THE MORE YOU TALK— THE LESS YOU PLAY

EVERYONE KNOWS that within the business and sports worlds, there are essentially two types of people: those who *take action* and those who *talk about it*. The talkers almost never get around to doing anything.

It's a tragedy to talk about things you never get to enjoy. What would you rather do, talk about eating a pizza or eat one? Talk about dancing or dance?

There is an ancient proverb: "He who talks much, says little." And those who talk about "doing it" often make excuses why they didn't do it and why they don't play anymore or participate in life. They have many entertaining stories about the past—the glory days that they no longer get to enjoy. And it is easy to get sucked into listening to their tales, because they possess the passion of yearning. Yet, do not be fooled: there is no glory in these history lessons that have dragged many down into the ranks of apathetic couch quarterbacks, who missed their chance to be a real one.

Those who talk about life need to taste it the most. They are craving it, yet at the same time, they try very hard to avoid living. Nothing demands more energy than resisting the fulfillment of your desires and destiny. It requires more to swim against the current than to float along with it. But for those who have the courage to live, to take a chance, to make mistakes, to sweat, to dance within the fire: for them—there is a taste of glory.

Affirmation

My blessed life is so magnificent that I need not talk about it or the lives of others.

THE DOOR IN
IS THROUGH AWARENESS

THERE IS A DOOR that leads through and beyond the mind. This door opens the way to the heart and consequently all other doors. The door has a name, one that upon first hearing it will sound trivial. It is not. It is the *key to all success*—Awareness.

All that occurs to you is perceivable only because of awareness. Without it you could not experience anyone or anything.

You can be aware of your body, mind, and consequently, the world only because of awareness. Without it, you could not perceive anything. For this reason, it should be your primary focus in life if you wish to succeed in all areas and realize who or what you truly are.

If you can become aware of the most subtle dimension, awareness itself, then the world is your canvas to paint on. To be truly aware of something, you are in control of it because then that thing has no power over you. To be aware of *awareness*, you have become aware of the stuff dreams are made of, consciousness itself, where all thoughts are arranged into your world. For this reason alone, if you are desiring the ultimate success and fulfillment, this is where you must begin.

This road to awareness can be accelerated a thousandfold through the practice of Self-inquiry: through asking yourself with each thought that arises, "Who is thinking?" The answer is, "I am." Because only you can think your thoughts. The real question, then, becomes, "Who am I?," doesn't it? Eventually, this question becomes a penetrating inquiry into the core of reality itself, so be ready.

At first, inquiring "Who am I?" will seem like a rudimentary question—because it is—yet it is this very simplicity that takes you straight to the heart. And it is the heart that leads to all other doors. So if you are ready for the true and direct path of the spiritual warrior, then awareness is the door.

Affirmation

I am the awareness within all existence.

WHAT YOU RESIST—YOU WILL NOT UNDERSTAND

WHAT YOU RESIST, you cannot see. Your very struggle prevents it. You may glance in the general direction, but it will be hiding in your blind spot. You will be looking, but only reluctantly. In the back of your mind, you will be waiting, hoping for something more desirable to come along. It is like fighting a headache, which only makes it worse.

As such, one's unwillingness to confront fears and weaknesses can become one's greatest debility. It is like going to the doctor's office to receive an injection where you reluctantly extend your arm, cringing in anticipation of the needle. This is like most people's lives because they fear many things before they actually happen. And once that *something* finally does occur, you usually think to yourself, "Now, that wasn't so bad." Yet beforehand, you trembled in anticipation of what would never happen.

What percentage of life is squandered by the expectancy of fictional mishaps that never occur? Sadly, it is during this interim that many postpone success indefinitely by resisting what they don't want, drawing the undesirable to them instead.

To transcend this pattern, awareness is needed. Awareness of what? Your Self! Because awareness— the antidote to resistance—is your most prized virtue. Acceptance works also, yet without awareness, you are blind: subconsciously resisting life while aimlessly stumbling in the dark, waiting for fate or somebody else to save you. Unlike a Hollywood ending, nobody comes. Why? Because they too are busy saving themselves, preparing for their own needle in the arm.

In any case, even if someone does show up to assist you during a crisis, they are only a temporary aid, like a baby walker until you develop the strength to walk on your own. If you look inside yourself, there may be some temporary fear or even resistance to this—yet only until you are freely standing without crutches.

The main question is this: does the resistance remain after the crutches are gone? Crutches are fine for those content to sit on the sidelines, but not if you want to play.

Consider Adrian Peterson of the Minnesota Vikings, who used his rehab from a torn ACL to become even stronger. No doubt many told him that he would not recover, yet he obviously chose to not agree with them.

Nothing anyone says about you becomes your reality unless you agree with it or resist it!

If you resist or push against something, it will push back, making it more real to you.

The most powerful person is one who does not resist anything. The universe is your mirror, so when you are non-resistant, the universe cannot resist you. Then you draw to yourself every desire of your heart.

Affirmation

Every situation reveals to me the wisdom to recognize life's perfection.

EVERY GAME IS A DANCE— UNDERSTAND THIS, AND YOU WILL NEVER LOSE

LIFE IS A DANCE, a natural flow. To be in the flow of life is like *being* the space that envelops a dancer while leaping and twirling, or *being* the lazy river that guides a floating log. The more you treat any action or event like a dance or flow, the more you are in complete control of a situation without even knowing it. This is the opposite of living in a state of anxious tension in want of control, where all movements are rigid and reflect a struggle. If you treat athletics like a dance, where you've become lost in the music— then you will not only dominate each match effortlessly, but also experience indescribable joy in the process.

Affirmation

I now open the way to flow successfully through life.

YOU CANNOT REALIZE WHO YOU ARE IF YOU'RE TRYING TO BE WHAT OTHERS WANT YOU TO BE

WHAT IS THE POINT of trying to be what others want you to be? What can be gained through it? At best, you will succeed at becoming their slave. Worst case, you will be utterly miserable and live a meager existence in service to tyrants. When you choose to play a sport, you must decide for yourself which role you want to play.

This much is certain: if you do not decide what you want to be, someone else will decide it for you. Is that really what you want? If not, then let your imagination soar! The joy of human existence is not just being alive somewhere—an insect can manage as much. Happiness requires you to express yourself.

Your destiny, your *position* in life, will serve all humanity and be exactly what your heart desires. In fact, it will be what you are most passionate about. It is for this particular reason that I am presenting this message to you here, that you may begin listening for your divine guidance that fills us each with Love, Truth and Purpose. Not the selfish purpose you have previously sought so you could merely survive, but that position on the team where all play together to unite with the universal brotherhood throughout the cosmos.

If you are uncertain what exactly that is, look within, and allow it to be revealed: *that* within you which is worth living for.

Affirmation

I hereby devote my life and everything given to me in service to All and realize who I am.

TALENT WITHOUT EXPERIENCE IS USELESS

WHAT GOOD IS POTENTIAL if you don't use it? You should exploit your own talents. If you don't, it is like having a Ferrari under a canvas in the garage so it won't get dirty. Experience is needed. A Ferrari was made to be driven. If you don't drive it often, then when you do it will get dings in it to remind you that nothing is permanent. All is impermanent.

It is essential to get this. Without experience, you're a mere statue, a lifeless chunk of cement. Like the living dead. Perhaps this is why people are so intrigued by shows about zombies, because they too feel half dead with one foot in the grave. Yes, they are moving, but that is not proof of living.

If a lizard's tail is severed and the tail continues to twitch, is it alive? No. And those who do not utilize their talents are as useful as a dead lizard tail.

What are you waiting for? It is simple: you are not waiting—you are hiding. Courage is needed. Some action is needed. So what are you hiding from? Maybe you are thinking that if everyone knows you have talent, they will admire you. But if you fail, then they will not think you are so good anymore and they won't respect you. Then the only logical choice is to not take the chance. Why risk it if many already think you are great: that you have incredible potential? At least then you are high on the pyramid.

Much like *Napoleon Dynamite's* Uncle Rico, you played one great game in high school, or perhaps you even set the state record. You are thinking, "Why not remain a legend?" Not so, because nobody has been thinking about how good you *were* since you left the field that day. In fact, even if you are still on the field, they will not be concerned about you.

Even if you break the world record, how much time will people spend discussing it or thinking about you? It is best that you do not squander your life away trying to impress others, because they don't care what you have accomplished. They are too busy leaving *their* own imprint in the sand. And soon, the ocean waves will erase you both. Not even a memory will be withstanding. So it is far more virtuous to enjoy your life, to celebrate each moment. That is what life is for—enjoyment! This is the mistake most people make: trying to live up to other's expectations. You cannot. Because if you do, they will expect it again. They will raise the bar for you over and over, so you must keep leaping through hoops like a dog. "That was easy, now perform for me again, Toto." They will say, "No, like you did it last time!" And they will be disappointed. You will become a show dog, a show piece. Your children will bring you to "Show and Tell" at school and you will be a huge success for thirty or forty children, until you walk out of the classroom.

The point is, no matter how good you become or how many championships you win, people will keep raising the bar. This reminds me of Lebron James in the 2013 NBA Championship. When being too generous with the ball, he was criticized for not shooting or scoring enough, yet if he scored too much, fans complained that he was being selfish. Such nonsense.

You can never satisfy people, so it is foolish to try to impress them. Even if you are the best in the world, announcers will begin comparing you with players from the past to create a competition between you. They can be dead for a century or more and still you will not be good enough to beat them in these people's minds. The inferior mind is constantly comparing with others—that is its M.O.

Now, I'm not saying don't play anymore; on the contrary, have unprecedented fun. In fact, if you are having fun, you've already won the game of life. And *when you no longer care about what others think of you*, then you can enter *The Zone* at will, but not until then.

So your participation and experience is needed to have fun, not the approval of others. A horse pent-up is miserable. A dog in a cage is depressed. They need to play. If they cannot, they will become ill and die. And so will you. Now (most of) these animals do not have the ability to go outside and run around without some help, but you do. Seize the day!

Affirmation

*I cherish each moment in life and easily fulfill my
divine destiny.*

NEVER OVER-ESTEEM OTHERS

IT IS COMMON FOR PEOPLE to admire the powerful, rich and famous. And since it's an accepted custom, few ever question their reasons for doing so.

It is a peculiar tradition because every athlete loses sometimes. Only when we acknowledge this and our individual sense of pride disappears can we truly know what happiness is.

Why would one ever worship another? When we over-esteem others, it cultivates a society of slaves, because if *they* are great, then *you* must be inferior by comparison—otherwise, why worship them? It is subtle, but nevertheless deeply rooted in the subconscious. Now, why would you want to set yourself below someone or above another? The answer to this question can be disturbing at first: if you worship or over-esteem others, it is because one day you too would like to be worshipped atop the pyramid. Why else would you willingly subject yourself to seeing others as superior to you?

The need to be seen as higher than others is ego, born of an inferiority complex. This need essentially cripples the potential for greatness. It's a paradox. You would think those ascending the ladder would become highly successful, but they will not. In fact, those who attempt to ascend are on a hamster wheel to nowhere.

For those who are already successful, what is their concern with the top or bottom? There is no concern. They are too busy playing and enjoying life to worry. Athletes who under-esteem themselves tend to over-esteem others. If you set anyone above you, then you set yourself below them. And if you over-esteem others, you and all others who look up to them become weak and powerless. Soon, you will think you are a victim. If this mindset becomes widespread, your team becomes weak, frightened and aggressive. Then you start bullying smaller people to assert power, all the while doubting your own.

It is the same for an athlete who sets out to defeat lesser opponents while avoiding those that are better. Perhaps you want to build your confidence by winning more easily, by huge margins—but you won't improve. There is a saying on the wrestling mat: "You have to take your lumps." Yes, you may lose every day for years, but in light of your humility, you will learn at such an accelerated rate that you will soon be a champion.

Put yourself not in a position to win, but to improve, and soon both will materialize. This is one of the keys to excellence—the willingness to lose while you are learning. You don't have to like it, but you must be willing, and you must never quit. In fact, you will be just uncomfortable enough to work harder, yet so focused on improving that you scarcely notice failure anymore. In this balance, failure falls away.

Most choose the quick and easy path of playing with those who make them feel or look good; yet this approach always fails to yield fruit in the long run, because you will acquire the habits, thoughts and attitudes of inferior players by playing with them. You will make the same mistakes they do and fail to experiment with new and more challenging skills, relegating you to lower levels of ability. Therefore, it is vital that you play with superior athletes if they allow you to. Yes, even if you are outright rubbish, do it! Especially then. And in time, the genius within you will emerge. What was once complicated will become second nature for you.

My friend, Otto Eichmann, often brought his younger brother, Eric, along when we practiced soccer. At the time, his brother was considerably smaller, but fearless. He was intent on keeping up, and he soon surpassed us both, later going on to play for the U.S.

Olympic and National Team. In time, he even qualified to play in Germany's coveted Bundesliga. This was unheard of for a U.S. player at the time and it is even rare today. Ask any professional athlete and they will assure you they wanted to practice with superior players when they started on their journey.

I have an unwritten rule:

> With the exception of playing for charity, *never watch poor athletics or play with low-level talent,* if you can at all help it—especially when you're in development. And make sure you know the difference.

Affirmation

I am effortlessly led to the victory beyond all struggle.

RETALIATION BLINDS YOU TO THE REAL PROBLEM

WHEN FOULED, there is nothing to say or do, and any retaliation reinforces your opponent's desire to do it again. Once realizing they have upset you, then it is only a matter of them doing it more effectively without getting caught.

When someone fouls you, they are expressing their own anger or frustration and confessing to their fear of you. If you remain calm and do not take things personally, you can play your game without any concern for others' actions. Yet if you react, they own you—and they know that they have found your button and they can push it any time they need to pull you away from your game and out of The Zone.

The more pivotal a player you are, the more significant a momentum shift due to a penalty can have on deciding the game's outcome. So what is the best way to handle being fouled?

If someone attacks you physically or verbally, simply ask yourself, "Who is getting upset?" The answer is "I am." Feel this "I." Then inquire, "Who am I?" Or, "What is this "I" that has become upset?" By giving attention inwardly to the sense of "I" or "I am," you instantly forget about the assault or that it even happened, and thus you go about your affairs, unaffected by the attempts of others to drag you down.

Realize this: most reactions to others are not generally a matter of life or death, but defending honor, whenever one has perceived oneself as being disrespected. Thus, any personal reaction by you is an egoic response, which will pull you into undesirable outcomes. This is why I suggest the above process of inquiring, "Who am I that is upset?" and turning your attention inward. Observe what happens. Retaliation always blinds you to the real dynamics of the situation at hand.

Bottom line: if your opponents are focused on stopping your team via foul tactics, they are playing to not lose. They are preoccupied with hindering you while you focus on scoring on them. Hence, the advantage goes to your team.

Affirmation

I realize that all adversity is a reminder to give my undivided attention to what I really want.

THE BETTER ATHLETE OFTEN LOSES TO ONE WHO DOESN'T KNOW ANY BETTER

When it comes to life, nothing is certain—yet in general, the average baseball player should defeat a good basketball player when playing baseball, based on experience alone.

Similarly, even when you play an opponent of superior talent, you can still win easily if you play *your game,* where it is creative and innovative enough and your opponent doesn't know your game as well as you. Look at it another way: it is like playing someone in an unknown sport, where you know the rules—and they don't!

If you stick to your game plan, your persistence, preparation and attention to detail will pay off and you will clearly recognize patterns that will give you the advantage.

Generally, only those who read or watch the news ever acknowledge another team's superior talent. This is why I recommend not reading anything about your opponent other than your coaches' own subjective scouting report. There is no need to set yourself against a sensationalized phantom image of them that does not exist. Stick to the facts and details of your game preparation; then your mind can become your ally rather than your enemy.

There is no such thing as an upset in sports, only mismatches, whereby you set your strength or strong players against the opponent's weaker ones. Individual mismatches spread throughout the court or field are cumulatively subject to spiritual law: what you think about becomes your reality. Your thoughts and attitude carry a far greater influence over the outcome of an event than someone's past reputation. All reputations are like history lessons—nothing but paper and ink from the past. It is false information because it is not here and now where the game is actually being played.

So do not be too concerned about body size when it comes to sports. Life has a way of balancing things out for us. Nature is a perfect example: how many tiny blades of grass survive devastating storms, where the massive trees lie in ruin? Also remember: contrary to cultural messages, the bigger athlete is not necessarily the better one. *Those who have true faith in life succeed where all others have fallen.*

Affirmation

My unwavering success is rooted in my knowing that I am one with all existence.

ACKNOWLEDGE WEAKNESS, CAPITALIZE ON MISMATCHES

THE SECRET TO DEFEATING a superior opponent is acknowledging your weaknesses and capitalizing on mismatches. What makes this strategy so effective is that most people are not willing to confront their fears. When the opposing team scores early or the clock is running out and a team is staring down the barrel of imminent defeat, most coaches and players become paralyzed, failing to recognize crucial player mismatches, which they might otherwise notice and exploit.

Now, what I am going to suggest here—with the exception of the fourth step—is not to be done under normal game circumstances, because it may potentially draw you out of your game, unless you or your team is highly disciplined.

One, find your opponent's two greatest weak spots (i.e., they don't catch well, they are inconsistent on three-point shots, they can't hit a curveball, they lack endurance or speed, etc.)

Two, focus the majority of your game plan on improving your execution in the two areas where your opponents are weakest. This will shift momentum by drawing them out of their strong game and into their weak one. How? They will recognize your team is strong in those areas, lose focus on what works for them and question whether an upset is possible. At that point, if you don't let up and your team is well-conditioned, the game is over.

Why two different areas of weakness? So if they manage to protect one, you can exploit the second and rebound back and forth.

Three, convince your teammates that your opponent's weakness is now your team's strength, and that they should work a new game plan: to draw your opponent into a situation favorable to your team.

Four, get each player on your team to repeatedly imagine how they're going to feel as time runs out and you've won big. This may seem strange to some, yet this is key, because this spiritual law requires you to live from the end of the movie, feeling your desired outcome until it manifests in your world. Thus, it is essential to keep the feeling of having already won in your team's consciousness.

Affirmation

I give thanks for my opponents playing at their best, elevating my level of play and assuring my success.

IF YOU'RE IN A SLUMP, FORGET THE PAST AND TAKE MORE RESPONSIBILITY

GOT SLUMP? If you fall into a slump, there is usually an individual sense of effort, an individual "me" trying to do it all. This temporary phase is a result of living in the past or being selfish.

A slump is all in the mind and can only exist if a current event is being compared to your past, a history that is nonexistent. So forget the past performances that once made you famous. Can you touch the past? No. It is a mirage—do not be seduced by it. What once seemed like a blessing can become a curse, because your mind will be constantly trying to compete with the memory and return there. Perhaps the experience was such that you surprised yourself, and you do not believe you can match it. While this is normal at first, do not believe it.

Realize that if you continue to play those old tapes in your mind, they will interfere with your here and now. Yes, you must let it go! If the media asks you about your player history, let them know that the past is over and you are not interested in memories or repeating it, only playing your best game now.

All record setting is for the fans, not the athletes themselves. So enjoy the moment and move on. *You can only evolve if you release the past, not before.* If you realize this, you will exceed your past accomplishments because you can now build on the wisdom you have acquired.

If you find yourself in a slump, get out of the "me" and into the "we." Find a way to serve the team. This deepens your awareness of The Zone and your connection with your environment. It is here that the bubble of frustration bursts and you release enough pent-up energy to catapult you into a vortex of higher expression. Be the We! Only the team player succeeds long-term with anything—and any team dominated by selfish superstars doesn't win championships.

> "Talent wins games, but teamwork and intelligence wins championships."
> —MICHAEL JORDAN

"Hogging the ball" is most common in basketball, soccer and lacrosse. To encourage teamwork, practice setting the team *ball hog* on one team in a scrimmage, and the rest of the players on a second team. This demonstrates how success is based on the integral support of all players contributing, even if only to spread out your opposition.

For example, in basketball, you may set five players against the individual player (a.k.a. the ball hog). All the teammates will learn their lesson, but this individual player must feel the detrimental impact of attempting to "do it all by myself." This is essential because not only do ball hogs usually think they are doing it all alone, they also put overwhelming pressure on themselves by trying to do it all. This is a stress that over time will take its toll on even the world's greatest athletes.

After the hog comprehends the lesson, let several other players also try to be the hog for a while, until the point is grasped collectively throughout the team. Let it be frustrating for the hog, but make it fun, allowing teamwork to emerge as the central focus. Emphasize passing with little to no dribbling or individual possession. This accentuates how individual players can only excel because their teammates, being marked by opposing players, prevent your challengers from swarming the hog and easily overtaking them. This lesson, effectively understood, will win you championships and save you numerous headaches along the road to glory.

Affirmation

I am always present to this moment and in harmony with my teammates, whereby we achieve the optimum result possible.

A FLEXIBLE MIND AND BODY IS INFINITELY CREATIVE AND EMINENTLY UNPREDICTABLE

WHEN THE MIND IS STILL, it is open to infinite wisdom. If it is rigid and stubborn, it will be closed, like a person who deadbolts their door shut, afraid someone will threaten their safety or take their precious possessions. Such people remain unable to receive the divine gifts entitled to them. As the closed-minded falsely believe they already know, they lose all their entitlements.

The inflexible mind usually accompanies an inflexible and tense body, where one then lacks the alertness and agility to avoid injury or maneuver. On the other hand, an open mind is creative and indefensibly unpredictable—traits common in all great athletes. Prescription: meditation and yoga.

Affirmation

I always function under the direction of divine inspiration, quickly making the best possible choice.

ATHLETES WHO USE DRUGS CAN'T TRULY BE CONFIDENT

USING SUBSTANCES TO ENHANCE performance is a risky business on many fronts beyond even health. Perhaps the greatest detriment of drug usage (prescription or not) is that it leaves a psychological residue of doubt, leading one to question their ability to succeed without the substance, should they ever decide to come clean. "If I quit, how can I compete with the bigger, faster, stronger and younger guys?" As a result, athletes who use drugs not only become dependent, but in most cases, they also feel a deep sense of guilt and the fear of getting caught, which over time does eventually manifest or take its toll.

This can be a monumental issue, because these suppressed emotions have become entangled in one's very idea of success and even their identity. Peculiar as it sounds, all who achieve extreme success will eventually have to confront their ego or be nudged off the pedestal they sit upon. You will either humble yourself, or be humbled—there is no escaping it.

Therefore, one must develop true confidence, which requires wisdom. It is checking your ego in at the door by surrendering all personal pride. From there, you may bask in union with the Divine without developing a false sense of accomplishment and pride.

Affirmation

I desire only that which life inspires in me to feel good about myself.

Chapter

29

NOTICE THE PERFECTION EVERYWHERE

TRUE CHAMPIONS RECOGNIZE each situation as an opportunity for improvement. Many have heard that Babe Ruth was not only the home-run king, but also the strike-out king. Yet seldom do we think about Babe Ruth striking out. Nor do we think about failure when we are considering Thomas Edison, whose experiment required a thousand attempts before his research resulted in the light bulb that changed our world.

True champions bide their time, conserving energy and delivering the correct burst at the precise moment it is needed. They are not lazy or careless, but know when to rest and utilize each moment. This is done by studying each situation and maximizing efficiency and power where and when it is needed.

Nature demonstrates this perfectly: consider the lion. It lies around in the shade for hours, carefully watching with relaxed alertness. Then, when the moment of instinctive opportunity abounds, it rises alertly, stalks its prey and seizes the moment. It does not roam pointlessly for hours on end, wasting precious energy needed for acceleration at "go time."

I'm not saying to lie around all day and move only occasionally to open the refrigerator. What I am saying is, work intelligently with poise and utilize your acquired wisdom and talents. Receive each experience graciously, for all incidents are a stone on your path to Truth, whether you're aware of it or not.

A wonderful illustration of this, though not a sports story, is that of two teenagers from *Britain's Got Talent*, Jonathan and Charlotte. Jonathan suffered due to severe depression. According to Jonathan, he had a weight problem. His body was large, so perhaps he believed he ate too many donuts or didn't exercise enough. This attitude would be quite normal under the circumstances. But this would be a very superficial assessment. In fact, when Jonathan walked across the stage for his audition, Simon Cowell commented, "Just when you think things couldn't get any worse." Jonathan's long, frizzy, black hair hung down over a tattered Jimi Hendrix T-shirt. He had clearly not dressed to impress. Yet the song that poured from these teens' mouths was a heavenly gift to humanity. I cannot even begin to describe it with due justice, other than to say we were witnessing a celestial event. In that moment, one could clearly see that every experience Jonathan had ever known in his lifetime—be it disappointment, sadness, hunger, happiness and depression—must have been perfect to pave the way for THIS rapturous moment in his life. Every cheeseburger or piece of "bacon and chocolate" he had ever eaten, presumably under some distressing anxiety over his weight issue, proved a benediction, nothing short of the Divine exploding through him. Indeed, each soda or muffin Jonathan had ever consumed shaped his body perfectly so it could become the conduit in this magnificent crescendo at that precise moment. Watching this, it becomes remarkably clear: every thing that ever happens is utterly perfect. This is undeniable proof that we haven't the slightest control over what is going to happen next in life...or why. The doors of heaven flung open, displaying this blessing of tremendous passion, such that you need not ever again question anyone's purpose in this divine plan—that of why we are precisely as we are.

If you look closely, we are all being perfectly groomed for our divine debut, prepared for when we can bow our heads in humility and ask to be used as an instrument in the Divine masterpiece.

Individually, both Jonathan and Charlotte were superb, yet together they were indescribable, as Simon's mouth hung open before saying, "You Jonathan...are unbelievable." Though Charlotte initially struggled, her voice not at its peak during the first audition, she marvelously raised the roof in the following round, muzzling Simon, as the two captivated the crowd.

Point being that, in any given moment, you may expand to reach a point of critical mass and reveal an explosive burst of pure expression. In this way, the Divine extends within itself like someone wiggling their fingers into a tight glove to gain greater dexterity of its extremities. You never know when it will happen. Life even utilizes so-called "flaws," like stones that allow us to walk over the stream to realize our ultimate perfection.

We must look for the perfection in every single instance. No single experience is the end-all destination on the road to success. Every athlete who has ever missed a last-second attempt or gotten ejected from a championship game knows this. Experience thus teaches us: what matters most is the ability to embrace both failures and achievements, which guide us onward to participate in the fulfillment of our destiny.

Affirmation

I am grateful for seeing the glorious perfection everywhere and in everything.

Chapter

30

EVERY THOUGHT AND ACTION IS AN INVESTMENT

IT MAKES THE GAME OF LIFE SO much more enjoyable when you understand the rules. Yet most people are completely unfamiliar with the powerful law that governs the universe.

What is the law? That each and every thought and mental picture you *hold* in your imagination is a coming attraction that eventually out-pictures the 3D reality known as "your life."

Many people steadily subject themselves to not only visual and musical forms of violence for shock effect, but also countless hours of destructive video games, media and misinformation for mere entertainment. This is not to say it is wrong, yet it poses a question:

If you knew that your thoughts were creating your reality, would you be making the same decisions in life?

It is spiritually essential that on your quest for athletic success, you understand the creative power of your awareness and thoughts. In other words, why give attention to potentially destructive thoughts when you can just as easily create a world of unlimited success and beauty?

Yes, it's true: what you think about grows into your reality. And when you are experiencing something, all your visual images and thoughts imprint a vibrational residue in your consciousness that eventually becomes part of your world. This means, quite literally, that you are the arbiter of your own fate. And when you know who and what you really are, life is a joyous, celebratory collaboration, not a punishment for past transgressions.

The more you practice creative visualization and succeed in manifesting simple things, the more you develop the knowing that you can create any reality you desire. Then, if you believe it in practice, it becomes natural for you to create anything you choose. Focused thought energizes and expedites creation. In fact, all apathy is just a lack of motivation stemming from being unfocused or unclear about what one wants. This is because apathetic people usually do not believe they can have what they want. Most people typically believe they are separate from what they are creating, which is simply not so. In order to effectively create anything, you must realize that you are molding yourself into what it is that you are dreaming—that you and your imagination are not two separate things. In fact, *you are your imagination!* You are the very substance that you are creating with. If you close your eyes, you can be aware of boundless space. *Try this now.* What this means is: your consciousness is boundless and unlimited.

Once in possession of this wisdom, you then have the capacity to purposefully create whatever you want. But if you think you are separate from that which you are creating, how are your thoughts crossing over from the mental to the physical plane? How can your imagination create anything in a world outside of you? How would the idea get from your consciousness to out there somewhere? That is unless the out there is really in you as your consciousness...unless everything is really inside of you. If you think that your thoughts project outward like waves, they must still be traveling through some form of medium. What is that medium? It is You. You are the medium—your consciousness is the screen on which all ideas take form.

Consider the scene in the movie *The Matrix,* when the small boy in the Oracle's office says,

"Do not try to bend the spoon, that's impossible. Instead, only try to realize the truth." "What truth?" "There is no spoon. Then you will realize that it is not the spoon that bends, it is only yourself."

Direct your attention to the image of what you want, realizing it is yourself, and you will become that. Your past thoughts have determined what you now have in your world, so it is not difficult to realize that your current thoughts will similarly influence what you will have in your world to come.

Give attention only to what you want, and never to what you don't want.

And *knowing what you want* is different from knowing how you'll get it. As such, it is not necessary to know how you will get what you desire in order to receive it—focus only on the feeling of already having it. Simply put, if you give attention to feeling happy and having fun, then all that gives rise to happiness and fun will emerge inside you—first, in your consciousness, and then in your world.

Affirmation

I treat every thought as an investment, attracting all that I want, such that my life explodes with success and prosperity beyond my wildest dreams.

YOUR DREAM FULFILLED IS THE DIVINE PLAN AND SUCCESS IS YOUR DESTINY

TO BELIEVE AN INDIVIDUAL has the capacity to fail or succeed based on what they do individually is like believing a cloud has control over its position in the sky. Even to pray for success is out of your hands, for you could not pray if it were not the will of the Creator. Omniscience is infinite intelligence—therefore, It knows precisely what you want before you ask.

You are ALWAYS precisely what the Infinite Source wants to Be when It is expressing EXACTLY what you are. The entire cosmos is an out-picturing of the eternal sacred happening where your true destiny is being revealed to you, gradually, as "your life."

Affirmation

I fulfill all my righteous desires unto my destiny, which is inevitable.

Chapter 32

TENSION ON IMPACT ONLY —THEN RELAX AND MOVE

TENSION AND RELAXATION are like sides of a coin. Without one, the other could not exist. Oddly, many suppose that there can be one without the other. A person may live for eighty years and still they are surprised when polar opposites occur in pairs. For example, human beings want pleasure but no pain; good but no bad, success but no failure, victory but no defeat!

How can you have one without the other? There is night because there is also day, tall because of short, fat because there is skinny and birth because of death. It is a confusing fact for some that if you want only pleasure, you will be very subtly resisting pain. So many become discouraged by the agony of defeat and quit sports altogether, hoping to find their niche in something else. Or maybe, as a child prodigy, you abandoned a promising future in music. One, or perhaps two failures, and you've hung up your cleats or violin for good.

It is foolish. Do you jump up and expect to never come down again? Everyone has been educated in these principles, yet still the truth eludes many. Sir Isaac Newton's second law of motion is the law of opposites: every action has an equal but opposite reaction. When night comes, do you not expect to see the sun's light in the morning? Failure to understand this is why it is acceptable for someone else to drop the game-winning touchdown, but not you. If it is someone else, you encourage them to never give up...but if it is you, then you will hide after the game. You'll go home to your room. You have come to accept failure with things outside you, but not for yourself. You want one side of the coin: all good with no bad, which sets you up for disappointment.

When failure has come to you, be prepared for great success—if you continue. If you have a pattern of quitting things when they go wrong, then you are making a big mistake. It is like exercising and quitting before your body shows improvement. Perhaps you work out for a week and cannot bench press your body weight, so you think you are weak. Forget the fact that nobody bench presses their weight after only one week. You have become impatient and so you miss the best part, harvesting the fruits of your labor.

Likewise, after tension, you should relax. And when relaxed, your body naturally begins tensing in preparation for the upcoming contraction or impact. It is normal. To human knowledge, expansion-contraction is everywhere throughout the universe.

When the body is tense or holding stress, your natural response should be to relax and gather strength. It is common sense. Yet, most people rest only during sleep and do not rest when they're awake. This makes one associate stress with being awake. Under such logic, you will be stressed out whenever you are not sleeping. So many athletes retain stress in this way and become exhausted.

If you do not consciously relax, when the time comes to exert force or accelerate, you will be unable. You will be pre-exhausted, so how can you? It may take a month or more to recover from exhaustion. Thus, you can see the dilemma when a breakdown occurs just before playoffs, or worse—during them. Balance is needed—tension and also relaxation.

I recommend silence. Some call it meditation, but it is really just sitting still and noticing life all around you. It is amazingly rejuvenating to be completely still and allow your mind to empty of thought, because all stress exists in the mind. Empty the mind and there is no stress.

I remember when my friends thought meditation was evil, a sign of the devil. But how can just sitting quietly be evil? Is sleeping evil too? Meditation is just like sleep, only you remain conscious of your existence, aware that you are aware. Understand, when you are able to relax at will, only then can you execute a task perfectly. When you can stop the mind on demand, then you can utilize the power of the mind on command; otherwise, you cannot.

Awareness of tension brings relaxation, giving rise to the no-mind state. To know the secrets of accessing stillness and relaxation provides you a key that opens every door in the universe. Practicing meditation, you are able to move powerfully with grace and precision, becoming even more intuitive and instinctive on the field.

Your ability to direct the mind and your attention anytime makes you like a god among men. This is akin to complete surrender: praying without ceasing. This requires the resolve to hold the mind and its mental impulses at bay. When you can do this, you are the master of your own fate because your consciousness will have merged with the Divine consciousness.

In such situations, you will be able to anticipate things a split moment or more before they actually occur, often providing you with a distinct advantage, what I call *The Edge!*

Affirmation

My mind is still and my body is at ease, so I joyously fulfill my purpose.

WHEN YOU PLAY AS ONE, YOU'VE ALREADY WON

Your greatest contribution to others, including your teammates, is to hold a visual picture of them that they want for themselves: this is the ultimate gift we can offer each other. Typically, as one gets too close to their own affairs, they become fearful and doubt their ability to succeed. Yet a true friend sees clearly their imminent success and never strays from that image of them.

This is the real secret of teamwork: *no one can fail, if even one other person sees them as already successful.* Such is the power of the collective vision.

Looking at history, countless people have owed their success to another person who "believed in them"—that is, someone who held a perfect idea in mind without wavering from the completed mental image of their success. This is extremely powerful, due to the fact that others do not see the limitations that we often hold about ourselves.

A good example of this is the Spanish National Soccer Team, having won some nine of their last fourteen international tournaments, as of this writing. Because like a family, they play with the unison of a single person's left and right hand. When people spend time together, they effortlessly begin to take on the same vibrational qualities and virtues. This is why many coaches schedule retreats for their players, traveling somewhere so the collective consciousness of the group is undisturbed by the masses, and awareness of their connection can deepen.

This unifying phenomenon is akin to how harmonics work: if you strike a tuning fork and hold it up to another of the same pitch, it too will begin to vibrate, having assimilated the frequency. And since all matter resonates an energetic signature, it is possible to propagate intelligence along these lines just by spending time in proximity to others who possess the qualities you desire. As such, if the players are functioning as a unit, absent of ego, then one player's entering into The Zone triggers a chain reaction that spreads throughout the team, and momentum is achieved. If this momentum is sustained, then victory is certain.

Affirmation

I enthusiastically participate in the dance of the Divine, sharing in our team's excitement and rejoicing in our success from playing as a single unit.

NOTHING EVER HAPPENS THAT WAS NOT NEEDED

PERHAPS THE MOST COMMON reason for error or failure is the regret over loss or dwelling on past mistakes. Yet, strangely, there is actually no such thing as a *past* mistake because there is no such thing as time—let alone a past. There is only the Now, where all is eventually revealed as perfect. For those who have gained access to The Zone, there is evidence of this timeless state of perfection.

Of course, we have all heard the statement, "Be in the Now." And in this now-ness, all that one can do is notice what is *always* here— the Truth.

Yet a forgetfulness of Truth on one's part does not constitute an error in what is True, does it? Nothing can ever change the Truth!

Put another way, could the Infinite Intelligence ever make a mistake? This is a foolish notion once you've experienced being in The Zone first hand. Having done so, you may ask yourself, what could ever happen that is not needed?

Because certainly the omniscient One does not err unless It wants to. In which case, it would not actually be an error, would it?

On the other hand, to an active mind, all seems imperfect. That is, nothing appears perfect to a mind attuned to looking for flaws. So all things that you initially consider "imperfect" can only appear as such because of your limited perception (i.e., if a person has poor vision, this does not mean the world is a blurry place). Yet, upon enlightenment (i.e., putting one's spiritual glasses on), all is revealed as the multidimensional expression within the divine plan. In which case, what could ever happen that is not needed?

We have all heard of those athletes who got injured, yet during their rehab they became stronger, which later led them to become better players. As such, the so called "unfortunate" injury became a blessing in disguise. Things are never what they seem to be on the surface; there is always a much deeper purpose, even though at the time you may not see it.

Affirmation

I live with complete faith, knowing all happens according to what is needed.

REMEMBER—
THE TORTOISE WINS!

WHAT CAN BE SAID ABOUT PATIENCE? Perhaps the best way to impress upon you its importance is to highlight some blunders associated with it.

Everyone is familiar with a batter who swings too soon on a change-up pitch. Or an illegal procedure penalty in football. Or where a distance runner kicks too early and dies out down the final stretch. Then there's jumping the gun in the 100-meter dash at the Olympics. And I'm not necessarily talking about seconds here, but tenths or hundredths of a second that can make the difference. The sports world is riddled with countless examples that demonstrate impatience.

An athlete's impatience can also result from the media and its hype in anticipation of their performance, where they eagerly await their opportunity with so much enthusiasm that, metaphorically speaking, they end up bumping into the door before they can push it open. Impatience not only results in being too early, but sometimes causes our being too late. Whether too early or late, it is still rooted in the same fear or performance anxiety. Either one is trying to get the jump on the competition or one hesitates in fear of jumping too soon. Perhaps there is no example more obvious than a race car that starts too soon or too late, where a tenth of a second can equate to multiple car lengths at the finish line.

In sports, this impatient sabotage pattern is often reflected in young athletes who start out *gung ho* in a sport, but lacking patience, they become discouraged when they don't master it immediately— so they quit! Strangely, this often happens with those who have the greatest potential.

So how does one acquire patience? Locate your center, or give your undivided attention to what is before you. This *cannot* be over practiced. It requires you to be fully present in the now, where there is no time. Exercising the awareness of presence naturally cultivates the habit of patience.

Affirmation

In true faith, I patiently await the inevitable success of each situation, regardless of how things may look initially.

TRYING TO BEAT YOUR OPPONENT—YOU HAVE BEATEN YOURSELF

IT IS A PARADOX and all paradoxes are both true and untrue. If you do not beat your opponent, then how can you win? And if you are not trying to win, then what is the point of practicing? The main point being: if you do not win, it is unlikely you will ever be recognized or noticed by scouts. Yes, it does seem this way at first to the beginner's mind. But winning is not the result of trying to "win." You win because you are being the best you can be, to the extent that winning occurs effortlessly.

Ever notice that when you try too hard, everything seems to go wrong? That the faster you try to run, the slower you move? Success must feel natural; it's not a struggle. This sounds contradictory because we all know that work is necessary to execute at an optimal level. Yet, it is the psychological stress of "trying to win" that tenses the body, making muscles contract involuntarily. When you play tense, everything is affected; from your field of vision to stride length to even the depth of your breath, restricting everything from your endurance to your recovery rate.

Aside from this, *mentally and emotionally you cannot beat someone else without defeating yourself also.* Why? One must look inward to understand the essential meaning of this statement. You must see beyond what is perceived with your physical eyes and sense it with your inner eye of awareness. Perhaps it is better to say "feel" rather than sense, however, it is not a physical feeling like touch. It is an apperception, beyond your senses. In the same way, you can feel when someone sneaks up behind you. We are all connected and nothing separates us from everything—quite literally. Yet, this nothing is really a something. It is foolish to think that just because you cannot see something that it is not there.

Just as tall depends on short and hardness depends on softness, so too does nothingness exist in contrast to something. In fact, when you have gained access to this inner dimension of nothing, you have gained access to everything, because the nothing contains the everything just as the sky contains the clouds.

All things are connected by the nothingness that

permeates them. Since all opposites are contained within themselves, if you try to beat your opponent, then you have already lost.

It is a conundrum, because not only is the thrill of victory there, but the agony of defeat as well. Why would you want to win unless you are trying to escape the fear and agony of defeat deep within you? What is it that makes you need to win so badly? This need, like roots, reaches deep down within one's own need for approval from others.

I have seen it time and again: people will obsess over winning until they forgive themselves for their failures. When someone releases their self-judgment, they are free to have fun. Like a child, they can play again and so they step onto the road to greatness, where one wins effortlessly without even having to try!

Affirmation

I effortlessly achieve success and fulfillment without concern for victory.

AVOID PAIN, YOU SUFFER; AVOID LOSS, YOU LOSE

AVOIDANCE DRAWS TO YOU the very thing that you resist. The more you resist pain, the more pain you attract into your experience.

Your very purpose for living is to experience life. How could it be otherwise, given that you are in fact—ALIVE! So when you avoid or resist a thing, the entire universe will draw more of it to you because your mind is filled with the thought of it. Whether for or against something, you attract it. Knowing this, why not use undesirable thoughts to get clear on what you do desire and then focus your attention there?

Still, many have learned to avoid pain by watching others' reactions to it. We can learn to face pain, to confront it outright—because every athlete will experience it to some degree. Similarly, if you avoid loss then you will draw loss to you. So, if you resist losing, it cannot be avoided. Do not believe me; look at your life and notice what has happened.

I actually have seen a parent hit their child for losing. From observing them, it was plain to see that both the parent and child were afraid to lose. When a parent wants their child to win badly enough, the child's loss is taken personally, as though the child is an extension of them. Meanwhile, the child wants to win, perhaps because the parent only gives them positive attention when they win, presumably bringing pride and honor to the family.

It is insane because there are infinite variables, over which you as an *individual* have no control. Truly, you have command over not so much as a single cell in your body, nor can you control a single thought. If you could, you would allow only pleasant thoughts and never unpleasant ones. Interesting to consider, isn't it?

Amusing, the things we have come to believe we have control over. So much that when we lose, we behave as though we should not have. Yet in competitive athletics, there is always a winner and a loser. If you both want to win, why should you always be the winner? Who determines it? Besides, you cannot assert you practiced more because the person who practices more does not always win. There is more to it—countless intangibles.

There are many ways of looking at loss. Losing can teach us a great many things, three of which are humility, perseverance and discipline. Losing can even give us direction in life. I was the goal-keeper in my very first soccer game and after allowing eleven goals in the net—quite a lot on any level—the coach had no choice but to put me on offense, mostly to keep me as far away from our own goal as possible! What happened then? I scored three goals in the next game and became one of our primary goal scorers.

Losing can give you direction, luring you away from failure and toward success. One sign of a champion athlete is the willingness to turn adversity into a positive. In fact, you can even use loss and failure to formulate a success strategy. We can use experience as life's constructive feedback, treating each loss like a single step in an experiment.

Removing the personal element from loss is essential in sports and every other area of life. One who feels guilty after a defeat, believing they personally lost the game, will also believe they personally won the game when the team is victorious. A true champion does not take things personally, not even blatant criticism.

I once heard, "In the whole history of humanity, nobody has ever erected a monument in honor of a critic." This is true primarily because it requires no intelligence to contrive an insult. A *master* musician does not criticize someone trying to create music—it simply wouldn't happen. They may give suggestions, but a true master in any field does not criticize because greatness exists largely in part due to recognition of the level of dedication required to synthesize a masterpiece. Sensitivity is paramount in creating beauty. Thus, those with wisdom worth listening to will not be insensitive. Whenever someone is critical of something in you, it is really an area in them that they are not yet willing to notice—usually because it is too painful for them to look at. So they will project onto others to avoid it until they have suffered to where they must then acknowledge it.

Do not place much, if any, value on what others think. *Give attention only to what you want and never to what you don't want* because what you think about grows into your reality. Focus only on the feeling of already being what you want to be.

Affirmation

I accept all life as it is, thereby effortlessly attracting to me all that I desire.

WHEN YOU DO WHAT YOU LOVE, YOUR DESTINY UNFOLDS

DOING WHAT MAKES YOU HAPPY aligns you with the divine plan. As the divine destiny of every being unfolds, they are in vibrational harmony with the whole of existence. This "resonance" is identical with truth, love and happiness. It is humanity's gift, a divine birthright that should not be wasted but pursued consciously. When one breaks free of a societal conditioning that insists they follow the mass hypnosis, they become accustomed to doing only what feels good to them rather than what is expected of them by others. At this critical juncture, one naturally gains access to divine bliss, fulfillment and the ultimate freedom: union with All Existence.

Affirmation

I rest in the Presence of Being, while my divine destiny unfolds before me in miraculous ways.

Chapter

39

GENIUS NEVER FAVORED THE MASSES

ALL CARRY THE SEED OF GENIUS within, yet it seems quite common for many to squelch the attainment of their dreams by not editing their mental activity. As such, the percentages who have fulfilled their potential is alarmingly low.

Of all the athletes in the world, how many would you say are truly geniuses? By genius I mean fulfilled and utterly happy. Because if one has not discovered the path to fulfillment and happiness, how intelligent can they truly be? They may have knowledge yet what can this give them but more mental activity, which is ultimately the source of stress and anxiety? Therefore, I'd say maybe one in a hundred-thousand express inner genius! It is my experience that those fulfilling their destiny owe their success to an open mind, unrestrained by beliefs, dogmas and philosophies.

Affirmation

I see only perfection as the genius within me is expressed.

THERE IS NO PRESSURE

YOU ARE NEVER UNDER PRESSURE.
What is pressure but a self-inflicted
fear projected onto an event? One
only has pressure if they believe they
may lose—if there is doubt. To affirm
there is pressure, you unnecessarily
introduce into your mind the possibility that you can fail and all that this
can potentially mean for you.

Would an adult feel pressure if
they were competing against a small
child? Of course not, it is absurd.

In contrast, one need not look any
further than Arnold Schwarzeneg-
ger's reply when interviewed before a
bodybuilding contest: "What would
Lou Ferrigno have to do to beat
you?" Arnold's response: "There is no
such thing." Now, this is significant
because his answer does not allow

even a fraction of the conversation to go there or energize the idea of him losing. This demonstrates that in Arnold's mind there is not even a possibility he can be beaten. He barely allows the question "What would...?" No, because the conversation is over, changed due to the power of his conviction and confidence. Thus, the details of what needs to occur for Lou Ferrigno to win never even enter the conversation because the context is an empty box. It has nothing inside, so there is no possibility.

Understand: *when you are confident, there is no pressure.* You have done your homework and completed your preparation so what pressure can there be? Sure, there is pressure if you did not train, but other than this, what can force you to have pressure? And there can be no relaxation with pressure, only awkwardness and poor timing. Understand, if you affirm that you have pressure, this virtually *guarantees* your failure.

A great player executes with precision while relaxed and alert, feeling no pressure. So if you feel pressure, you are in a slump. Perhaps there will be an adrenaline rush if you need to get one more home run for the all-time record. Or if you're kicking a last-second field goal in the Super Bowl. Yet, even then you are prepared so you are really just there as an instrument. The pitch—the swing; the snap, the hold—the kick. All is just happening but you are not really there. It is just taking place and somehow you are there, yet you are not doing anything. Somehow the Divine has done it using you, but you did not do it personally.

In a game, you do not have time to think or "do" anything. Maybe you are aware of some pre-game jitters or butterflies, but once the game starts and you drop into The Zone, all of that comes to an end. Perhaps butterflies endure a bit if you are an inexperienced athlete, but not for an elite athlete. There is no time to think—and if you do, someone will steal the ball from you, you will trip over it, or you'll drop a wide-open pass in the end zone. You will miss an open goal or a layup in the closing seconds. Your ten-inch putt to win the Masters will spin off the lip of the cup. But there is no pressure for a seasoned athlete in The Zone. If you look like you are under pressure, the manager will either cut you or have you escorted to a psychotherapist so you will not feel pressure anymore. But therapy will not work, because talking will not erase your fear. Only looking deeper within yourself will accomplish this.

When I was a place-kicker, it was suggested that I take a meditation class. So if I ever would have missed a game-winning field goal, I could never use the excuse, "Well, coach, I was under a lot of pressure." No excuse is necessary if you fail because what is the point? Sometimes you fail, sometimes you miss—it is a fact of life.

You must understand that there is no pressure except in your mind. Yes, there is pressure in the mind, but not otherwise, so get out of the mind.

If you're playing, enjoying the game and not worried about landing an endorsement with Nike, Adidas or Gatorade then there is no pressure. But if you are worried about how good you look or how you're going to negotiate the big bucks, your mind will not be centered on where you currently are and what is happening. You will not be in The Zone. The Twilight Zone maybe, but not a peak-performance Zone.

Pressure only arises if you suddenly become frightened and you fall out of The Zone, but not while you're in it. And if you are aware of pressure, find out who is under pressure by inquiring, "Who is thinking they are under pressure?" At this point, you look back toward yourself and feel "I am." With this, you ask yourself, "Who am I?"

The pressure ends there, with the inquiry: "Who am I?"

Affirmation

I am.

41

THE ZONE IS FEELING THE SPACE AS YOURSELF

THE ZONE is a spaceless and time-less phenomenon. And how can you feel the intangibility of such nothingness? You must allow the invisible feelers of your awareness to extend outward; only then can you access the interconnectedness of all things. It is so elusive that trying to describe this subtle dimension escapes even those who frequently gain access to it. It is a shift in one's attention from what is here physically to what is not physical: *to That which sees, yet is unseen.* In a sense, you are there in the space yet you are no longer a thing and have no shape. You are a presence yet now your sense of Self seems to have per-meated everything.

When aware of The Zone, you do not need to do or have anything in particular, yet you accomplish actions perfectly, attracting the life of your dreams to you effortlessly.

Perhaps you recall making a perfect shot or play, moving in such a way that you never had before. In these moments, it's as though your body is being animated by some omnipotent force. Being in this state of relaxed alertness, you do not care what happens. So deeply rooted in the present moment are you that thoughts of what is going to happen next simply cannot arise. Initially, this can be difficult to comprehend because life, for some, has become a continuously worrisome burden—a perpetual anxiety attack. This, because the habit of worrying about the outcome of events has been conditioned deeply into your mind.

The solution or key to this is *shedding all you have learned and practicing being in the moment—* this moment! This means establishing a habit of giving your full attention to what is before you *now* without allowing distractions—for any reason.

Affirmation

As I align with The Zone, my desires are fulfilled effortlessly.

Chapter

42

CLEAR INTENTION AND RELAXED ACTION DRAWS OUT THE MASTER

To DRAW OUT THE MASTER in you is the ultimate task. And there is only one Master—Life. So, how then can you accomplish this if the mind is burdened with many thoughts that prevent you from accessing the stillness of divine consciousness?

First, you must realize that the entire universe wants to be utilized by you. Therefore, how can you be stopped? You cannot be stopped—you can only be detained by stubbornness, pride and egoity. Yet your ingenerate nature of perfection courses throughout every cell of your body and you need only to get out of the way.

Imagination is your true power source. It is the life and resurrection of your dreams. So, joining forces with the source of all creation, by setting into motion your clear intention of what you are wanting, you can then allow the Master to emerge from within and accomplish what it was meant to through you.

Affirmation

My mind is fully absorbed in the presence of the Divine, so I always fulfill my desired intention.

Chapter

KEEPING YOUR AGREEMENTS IS THE KEY TO SUCCESS

KEEPING YOUR AGREEMENTS is the key to a fulfilling life. Few people understand the true importance of agreements yet they are crucial to your success. How? They remove confusion. Because wherever confusion exists, there is a disturbing sense of agitation and stress that robs us of our happiness.

Agreement is the primary unifying arrangement, like an invisible cement between two or more parties that sustains our physical reality. People who keep their agreements are said to have integrity.

If you have integrity, you say what you mean and you mean what you say without making any excuses about why you cannot complete what is agreed upon.

The true dawning of integrity is apparent when arrogance disappears and humility arises. When people have integrity, they feel connected with life. They do not see themselves as separate, superior or deserving special treatment.

Without agreement, how could you ever meet anybody at a specified location, coordinate schedules or even go out on a date? If you don't keep your agreements, people won't be clear about what you want in life or how to accommodate you.

Some examples of agreement are the understanding by which you wouldn't pet a great white shark or cross a busy street without looking both ways first. Agreements are a general comprehension of how to perceive this physical reality, phenomena and the physical laws of the universe. This includes executing a certain play you and your teammates are performing.

Quantum physicists now agree that the physical universe is actually more like a holographic matrix of images seamlessly interwoven together by a network of understandings or agreements. So, without agreement to sustain the universe's structure, the order and function of our life would yield an impossible state of affairs; nobody would know where they are or what they are doing.

Most people depend on *time* to function in the world. If nobody agrees on what time it is, then what time would it be? What we call "time" exists only because of agreement!

If people didn't manage their time or keep their appointments, you would eventually have to stop making appointments just to avoid *dis*appointment. Without agreements, you'd be unable to meet at a location or communicate a mutual purpose.

How consistently people keep their agreements reveals their intelligence because those who do not understand the necessity for all beings to communicate harmoniously through agreement are simply not going to recognize the disharmony of their own life.

People's integrity informs you of useful information as to whether you should associate with them. This is true mainly because if people do not maintain their agreements, you will become confused about your relationship with them and feel a disharmony with life. Since our world is like looking into the mirror of our own consciousness, if people are breaking their agreements with us then it is certain that we are also breaking our agreements with them.

THOSE WHO KEEP THEIR AGREEMENTS USUALLY GET WHAT THEY DESIRE IN LIFE AND THOSE WHO DO NOT KEEP THEIR AGREEMENTS SELDOM GET WHAT THEY WANT. AS SUCH, IF YOU WOULD LIKE YOUR DESIRES FULFILLED THEN IT IS ESSENTIAL THAT YOU KEEP ALL YOUR AGREEMENTS!

Affirmation

I keep all my agreements and live a perfectly harmonious life, always receiving what I want.

44

IF YOU ARE THE CENTER—
THE GOAL IS EVERYWHERE

CONSIDER AN UNCOMMON NOTION: you are existence and your experience is like a sphere around you, where you are at its center. Now imagine that wherever your body moves, this sphere moves there also, always surrounding you. It is a massive space that includes all you can perceive with your physical senses. Then, stop. Take a moment to feel yourself as being the center of all your experience. Perhaps you may wonder how it is, that having lived for so long, you've never really felt aware of yourself as the center of life.

Of course, you have heard the words, "They are so self-centered." In fact, it is usually posed as an insult or criticism, yet that is not what I mean here. I'm not saying be selfish—on the contrary. Allow me to explain, because many have tried to comprehend this and not understood. Being in this sphere I speak of, consider where the center of the sphere *ends* and where the rest of the sphere *begins*. You see, there is no clear line of delineation between the center of the sphere and the rest of it. Expanding outward from the center, where precisely does the center end?

In your case, you are the center of your sphere of reality and your perceivable experience is the *inner volume* of space within this vast sphere. The difference between the sphere and your actual reality is that there can be no outer perimeter to life, no boundary to your awareness, which—if you will look into It—is infinite, having no limit whatsoever. And when you consider It, there is no point felt as me, no center point within you that you can point to and declare, "This is *me*."

You are the awareness. There is no division between you and your environment, *no* center as "you" *and* a separate existence "outside you." Indeed, nothing is separate from anything else in all infinity. When nothing separates you from everything, you are everywhere, including the space around your body.

It may take a couple once-overs to understand this, yet you must realize that you are not separate from any target or goal you are ever trying to hit. The target and you are no more separate than infinity is from your body. This being so, how hard is it for you to have your hand do what you'd like it to do—to pick up an apple or fork? Not difficult at all. It is simple, because you have spent an entire lifetime affirming and reinforcing that you are your body and that your hand is part of you. Where this understanding becomes critical is when you are willing to affirm that you are everywhere and everything, instead of just your body. Imagine the ramifications such a realization could have on your game and your life. To know that you are not a person, but one with all existence.

Affirmation

I am grateful for steady Self-awareness and the inspired manner in which I realize I am one with all.

Chapter

SUCCESS IS ACCOMPLISHING THAT WHICH YOU CONVINCED YOURSELF WAS DIFFICULT IN THE FIRST PLACE

THE HUMAN CONSCIOUSNESS is so powerful that, if you don't imagine or convince yourself that you're limited in some way, your consciousness will expand outward to infinity. It is true: you must actually convince yourself that something is difficult so you can then entertain yourself by trying to overcome your own thoughts about who and what you are. Hence, multitudes of people sit around cooperatively creating their own limitations so they can have something to overcome. It is quite humorous if you stop to consider it.

The real You is actually so unfathomably powerful that when you consciously drop into the state of unified consciousness—*a.k.a. The Zone*—you can accomplish unspeakable feats far beyond most people's own preconceived belief in themselves.

Therefore, the key to success is to stop convincing yourself of these imaginary limitations and rejoice in the glory of all that is before you. Treat each situation as a heavenly reminder of who you really are and utilize each by imagining what can be accomplished through you.

Affirmation

I confidently fulfill my every task and know my success is certain.

Chapter

YOU CAN ONLY LEARN WHEN YOU REALIZE YOU DON'T KNOW ANYTHING

SUCH IS THE PARADOX. How can you, whether in sports or life, learn something in the first place if you are admitting you haven't learned anything yet? You are saying, "All I have learned in the past was of no use whatsoever, because I no longer know it." And it is true: you do not know anything—in fact, you cannot!

Allow me to explain. There is a saying: "You can never step into the same river twice." On the most basic level this sounds absurd because of course you can. Well, the banks of the stream may not have moved but the water, like life, is in constant motion. It is constantly changing. What was true yesterday, one hour or even one second ago is no longer there. These changes may be imperceptible or even unsubstantial to you, yet nevertheless, they exist.

Socrates was once selected as the most intelligent man in all of Greece. It's true and reportedly when the news was released a furious outrage echoed throughout the Grecian halls of knowledge. Dozens of philosophers and theologians, who vied for recognition as the notable thinkers of their era, disputed that such an honor should not be bestowed upon such a low-caste individual. A large group even assembled before the committee, outraged: "How can you give such a prestigious award to him when he has outright declared that he does not know anything?" A board member responded, "Yes, it is true." The crowd quieted, sensing the board had finally come to their senses. Then the chairman declared, "And that is precisely why we selected him."

Only fools declare they know something outright. Anyone who has looked deeply into their mind realizes that all knowledge is relative and hence unknowable. A famous Indian sage named Ramana once said, "All knowledge is learned ignorance." Once you realize that nothing said by another can be the Truth, only then can you realize the same is also true for you.

So what can you learn? That knowledge is not something universal or to be acquired and hoarded, but rather to be applied to life and experienced— only then may it one day become wisdom. What will those who fancy themselves as more knowledge-able want to do with this information? They will argue and stay lost in their need to be right because, for them, their intellectual pride is more important than being happy.

You already know that which you need to know. What is that? When the situation arises, you will know precisely what I mean and what to do. Only one thing is changeless: formless awareness. Then again, awareness is not a thing. It is the whole of existence, the Source of Infinite Intelligence. As such, if awareness wants to change, it simply takes form. This must be acknowledged and understood because when the spirit is non-expressive—an infinite potential—then it is not changing. But when it is changing, it is no longer a potential. It has become a movement in consciousness, which expresses in this world as a finite thing or thought. That is all that can be said about it. Any more and we have diluted the understanding.

This is precisely why nobody has ever seen "God," at least not as a separate object. Why? Omnipresence cannot be seen because it is spread out everywhere. And if It is infinitely vast, then It is infinitely thin also—so how can It be visible? And if you are every-where, how can you see yourself? You cannot. Just as the eyeball cannot see itself and the knife blade cannot cut itself. Therefore, the phenomenal uni-verse is not here as a choice, but as a necessity, an ingenerate out-picturing of the Infinite. Much in the same way the sun gives off light, not because it tries to, but because light is its nature and it cannot help but radiate itself. So too, the Infinite presence expresses all that Is without the slightest effort whatsoever.

For infinity to know itself, it must become a subject and object expressing in time and space. From there, other things arise in response to the already existing duality. Where there was once only no-thing, there emerges a finite some-thing. And eventually, many things—countless things. Infinite things and universes. There is no end to things and their relationship to one another, so change is inevitable. And since change and impermanence is the only physical certainty, we must accept the fact that we don't know anything. Not knowing is the impetus for the Divine to show us Who and What we really are.

As an athlete, once you acquire the humility to admit you do not know anything, you are no longer committed to playing in the old way. Only then are you free to explore new things and evolve in both your play and intelligence. Only then will your creativity explode through the roof such that nobody, including you, will know how you are able to do things you now do. You will accomplish tricks and movements that surprise even you. With this dawns the realization that the Divine must be doing everything and that It has been all along.

Affirmation

I am one with Infinite Intelligence, and everything I ever need to know is supplied when I need it.

ALL SEEMING MISTAKES ARE BUT FORKS IN THE ROAD

THINGS ARE NOT WHAT THEY APPEAR. Though we often assign labels such as *success, failure* and *mistake* to different athletic situations, it is important to understand that all such designations and assessments are only superficial. On the deeper, more conscious level, there is only the perfection of the Divine playing out its drama. To think otherwise would lead to the belief in sin and then consequently, the idea that the omniscient Source could ultimately fail. Buried beneath the concept of sin, there is the notion that you are imperfect—that Source has created all there is, including imperfect beings. This erroneous notion must be contemplated in order to be free of ego and fear. Then, there can be no such thing as a mistake or failure—only one's limited vision of the bigger picture.

Now take, for instance, a person who builds a computer that runs a faulty program. Whose error is it? The computer's or the designer's? It is the designer's error because the computer is merely running a program. In fact, if you listen to most people talk with one another, it is obvious that they too are recycling the same conversations and programs over and over again like a computer—unaware they are even doing so. Most of our inner dialog is 99 percent repetitive. This unconscious patterning is evidence that your body-brain organism is just a machine, merely fulfilling its divine purpose precisely as it was programmed to.

The legendary Socrates asserted that nobody willingly chooses to do wrong—that doing wrong always harmed the wrongdoer, that nobody seeks to bring harm upon themselves, and that all wrongdoing is the result of ignorance. Therefore, as he concluded, it is impossible for a person to willingly do wrong because their instinct for self-interest prevents them from doing so.

The only other consideration is to believe that the Infinite Intelligence is capable of error, which interestingly enough, is a human projection. Remember, Infinite Intelligence simply cannot make errors, unless It wants to. In which case, it is not really a mistake! Is it? Even if one were so daring as to assert the idea of individuals having free will, where is the proof of an individual that is separate from the Infinite? And from where did they receive this free will? Then also, in which environment would they enact their free will? Can you have control over your entire environment? Do you have control over the thoughts that spontaneously pop into your mind? If so, then why do you have thoughts that you do not desire? Why not have only pleasant thoughts? These questions must be answered to justify a belief in free will and, thus, the notion of a "mistake."

Even if an alleged mistake occurs—whether one improves upon or complains about it—it is simply the result of a conditioned pattern running within a genetically programmed machine. Ergo, you have no control—it is an egoic fantasy. This recognition on the deepest level puts an end to ego: *the thought that "I have volition independent of Existence itself."*

Do not believe me. One should question everyone and everything. No concept, belief, dogma or doctrine is beyond reproach. Since this is a concept, please dissect it if you can. Until you learn to discern what is true for yourself, any attempts to improve will be based on what someone else wants for you rather than what you truly want.

At any rate, if an error is made, you will either eliminate the error in the future (if you want to improve) or you will make excuses for why you failed and continue to make the same error. Your path depends on your specific organism, its brain and its conditioning. People are eminently predictable, as the advertising industry has proven repeatedly. In fact, they can determine, within a percentage point or two, how many consumers will buy a product they are promoting.

Another thing: don't focus on errors, correct them, because what you think about grows and what you give attention to repeats itself. You only stand to benefit by giving attention to those areas that bring success, rather than dwelling on past errors. The more you think about errors, the more deeply they become embedded in the subconscious and replicate themselves in your experience—until you literally change your mind.

Notice the wonderful feeling of focusing on success and let this be your guide. There are only two basic types of experiences in life: those that feel good and those that do not. Those that feel good *will* lead you down the path of happiness and those that don't feel good *will not*.

Affirmation

With each experience, I improve, joyfully expressing the perfection of my destiny.

Chapter

KEEP YOUR EYE ON THE BALL AND GO TO THE TARGET

COACHES SAY IT ALL THE TIME, but what does it really mean to keep your eye on the ball? To stare at it, fixate on it and block everything else out? No. Because all attempts to block out the world—to avoid your environment—are impossible. In fact, by trying to keep the world out of your mind, it agitates the mind with even more thought! So do not block out the world—include the world. Feel it!

Observe Rannulph Junah, Matt Damon's character in *The Legend of Bagger Vance*, when his caddy urges him to *see the field*. And while you are feeling your surroundings, look on the ball with soft eyes. You are seeing it, yet you are relaxed and fluid. You see the ball, yet you are not really trying to look at it. Your body is firm and powerful, not stiff or rigid. Then, when you see the ball moving closer to you, or you toward it, you remain relaxed until impact. On contact, yes, you tense and transfer force into the ball, but the release is instantaneous. Tension is needed only for a moment…then it is suddenly not needed anymore.

Remember this: when you strike something or shoot a ball, you move through it totally, your entire body toward your target. Conserve nothing, suppress nothing: whatever you save—*you lose*. When this is done, faith is at maximum and you essentially *explode* without regard for making or missing your target. Even to say "your target" is not accurate because when you disappear into the moment, who is there to find a target?

They are two parts of the same phenomenon: you and the target. You cannot miss because the two parts are the same, mere extensions of each other. You are your own target in that sense. So, let it happen, do not make it happen. It wants to happen; it is ready. The stage is set, so enter and play your part, but nothing more. Do not try even to take credit for success because it is not your achievement. It is the entire universe moving through and animating your body. You are merely watching and allowing. If you try to do it individually, you will fail, and in doing so you have missed the entire point and the glory will elude you once again.

Notice that the all-encompassing presence of the Divine is doing it through you. Empty yourself for a moment, just for an instant, and you will feel the benediction, the glory of it all. You will not ever want to be there again as an individual. Eventually, you will realize there is no need for an *individual* you; only your awareness is needed. Only then can you totally disappear. Where you end and experience begins will become a blur—a virtual mystery to you. This is the beginning of life. It is what I mean by living on the edge of glory.

Affirmation

I abide eternally in the flow of Life, and with the utmost faith, I achieve perfect results.

Chapter

DO NOT BE FOOLED BY THE DARKNESS BEFORE THE DAWN

ENTERING THE FLOW of life is no easy accomplishment for the average person because conflicting thoughts, doubts and fears often surge up from the subconscious. This is precisely why it is said to be "darkest before the dawn."

This is a time when you must make your affirmations repeatedly and rejoice, giving thanks that you have already received. You can only receive that which you can see yourself receiving. That is, you can only attract that which is within your own mental picture.

Every great accomplishment has been brought into outer manifestation through holding fast to one's vision, and often *just* before the big achievement comes apparent failure

207

and discouragement. But never mind these diversions, because the athlete who understands spiritual law is undisturbed by appearances, and rejoices even while "yet in captivity."

So hold to your grandest vision and give thanks that the end is fulfilled, that you have already received. Your clear vision must pierce the world of matter and see clearly beyond the physical world into the heavenly dimension beyond form, where things are perceived as they really are—perfect and complete. Therefore, hold the vision of your journey and demand the manifestation of that which you know you have already received.

Now, what exactly do I mean by "the darkness" and "the dawn"? First, the dawn. The dawn is the fulfillment of your heart's desire, your arrival at the front doorstep of your life's purpose. The dawn symbolizes the culmination of a human's lifetime of efforts to discover what is meant to express as not only a joyous celebration, but fulfillment of one's destiny and service to all.

Just prior to this dawn, however, there is often an extended period of what can justifiably be called the darkness. This darkness symbolizes the interval that follows planting your seeds of desire. Once you have set forth a desire, you await its sprouting into outer manifestation—the eventual out-picturing into this physical world. This span of uncertainty, associated with waiting for the seeds to penetrate the surface and become visible, is what I call *The Gap*.

The Gap is the interval between your deliberately giving attention to your dreams and the actual manifestation of them as a physical reality. It could also be considered the duration required for your dreams to crystallize into a solid thing.

I am addressing The Gap here because, during this interval, people often become frustrated or doubtful that their idea will ever actually become a physical reality, and so they often give up, lose hope and settle for less than their ideal. It is during The Gap *interval* that people tend to allow sabotaging thoughts to accumulate, eventually weighing down and sinking their creative ideas, often just before they come into fruition.

It is absolutely essential that you be patient during The Gap, knowing that your dreams are already on their way or in the process of expressing from the moment you deliberately think them. However, we sometimes doubt this because ideas in our imagination appear to take time to manifest into physical things. But this can also be a fortunate thing because we sometimes have thoughts we'd rather didn't manifest. This buffer in time allows you to change undesirable thoughts, molding them into more desirable ones. Once you begin to visit your imaginary world more frequently, you will notice that your visions progressively evolve into more detailed scenarios. The more elaborate they become and the more senses they involve, the more believable they become…until you may even forget you're imagining these ideas and believe they are physically here now. Sometimes you may even become startled when you suddenly fall back from your imagined state into so-called "real time."

At this point, when you're unable to distinguish between what is *real* and what is not physically here, your idea is very close to manifesting in your world and you are nearing the end of The Gap. Yet be prepared, for the limiting thoughts that once prevented your desires from manifesting will surface. This is your opportunity to accept them and realize that they are not real, but shadows—nothing more than an opportunity for you to revise the coming attractions of your world before they materialize.

If limiting thoughts arise, watch them without reacting, then let them go. Once this pool of limiting thoughts empties—your dreams effortlessly emerge. How? Because your dreams are already here, right now! Even if you cannot see them yet, they are already here.

In The Gap, you find the weeds of limitation surfacing as they are expunged from your consciousness before the actual blossoming of your ultimate dream. During which time, you must face your deepest fears, doubts, temptations and inclinations to compromise and follow the dark side. This is "the dark night of the soul" prior to one's divine fulfillment. It is precisely when one must have faith and be watchful of any interfering thoughts, knowing and remembering that this phase is temporary. This period occurs just prior to the blessing you have prepared for throughout life. When making demands upon the Divine, you must prepare for the unexpected. Remember, everything may appear to be falling apart, when in actuality, it is coming together!

Affirmation

I see only the light of consciousness beyond illusion and appearance.

FIND OUT WHO YOU ARE, AND EVERYTHING ELSE RESOLVES ITSELF

THIS IS NUMBER ONE—The Key to all success: finding out who you really are aside from all the distorted concepts and beliefs you have inherited. And contrary to what you may have learned, there is actually a definitive way of realizing who you are beyond your physical body.

The irony is that what you find is not really an answer—at least not in the traditional sense of the word. It is more like a revelation or perception. Since the very core of who you are is often obscured by thoughts and emotions, we must approach this from a quite different avenue than we might typically look at things.

What are the means? By asking, and then considering the primordial question, "Who am I?" The answer to this question is not usually obvious at first, obscured by a myriad of thoughts. In order to "Know Thyself," it is essential to drop behind the mind into the space beyond it known as consciousness. This is accomplished by addressing each thought you have with the question: "Who is thinking?" The answer is always, "I am." Why? Because who else can be aware of your thoughts but you? Now since "I" am thinking, it is paramount that you inquire: "Who am I?" or "What am I?" Investigate—what is this felt sense of "I" or "me"? Few actually get around to considering it, though it essentially answers every question you have ever had. We all use the word "I" hundreds of times a day, yet what is it? What is this "I"? Most people abandon the search because they are too impatient to wait for the response.

You must look deeply within yourself for this silent, yet all-pervasive answer. And when this discovery is made, you will realize that everything in your life is already being taken care of for you, that it has always been taken care of. This answer will not be an intellectual one, or a booming voice from the clouds, but a simple knowing— beyond comprehension. As such, you must look for yourself because all verbal descriptions fail. You must find out directly. And when you know this, you will know all that is worth knowing.

Affirmation

I am forever surrendered to the glory of life.

YOU ARE WHAT YOU EAT

I CANNOT IMPRESS enough upon you how important what I am going to say here is without the following prelude.

Making wise food choices and drinking quality water *significantly* influences your athleticism, intelligence and thoughts, which govern the precise circumstances of your life. This is because every action is determined by a thought and each thought corresponds with a specific experience.

Your participation at the higher levels of athletics depends on many factors that collectively determine your overall success. Many justify practicing some of these, while rationalizing why they do not do others. Making wise food choices should be a priority. For instance, if you give attention to only fourteen of the twenty most important factors necessary to be an elite athlete (see Appendix B), then you can only expect to be approximately 70 percent of what you could have been had you prepared in all areas.

So here it is: in my direct experience, nothing hinders one's performance like being dehydrated and eating processed sugar, flour and high-fructose corn syrup. As usual, do not believe me—observe your body; let your life be a testament to the truth.

Now this is where we run into a paradox: you must be sensitive to recognize that your body communicates with you, yet you can only receive this information if your body is sensitive enough to where you are able to make the recognition. To begin cultivating this sensitivity, I suggest eating lots of fruits, nuts and vegetables, while also drinking very good quality water.

Most people have become lazy with their food preparation and rely on people they don't even know to determine what they're putting into their body. Ever consider why a home-cooked meal can feel so good? Because when someone who cares about you is preparing it, they are infusing it with loving attention. Yes, you really are what you eat in this sense: your body retains the energetic imprint and emotions of those who are preparing your food. And love is the most powerful food there is!

Now the straight and phat: most people will disregard what I am saying here. Their attitude will be, "I have done 95 percent of what you asked me to do, so who cares if I skip this one small thing and eat some candy, chips or soda?" No worries, but just remember that a committed athlete will do whatever it takes—this usually means the opposite of what is easy, what most people are not willing to do. This is why there are only one or two dozen athletes who get to play at a time, while thousands of people watch them from the stadium. And the better you become, the higher those numbers climb into the millions of spectators via Internet and television...because by then, you've already made the cut, the decision to walk the road less traveled and be your very best.

The elite athlete always takes necessary measures to ensure that what they are doing will optimize their potential—you owe it to yourself. It's easy to do what the majority of people are doing, but if you take the lazy man's path, don't be surprised if in a few years you're watching some of your old teammates playing on TV, while you sit around convincing your buddies how you played with those "who made it big!" There are no excuses that give you a second chance. Now is the time. This is the chance you've been waiting for—Seize the Day!

TOP 20 SIGNS OF
AN ELITE ATHLETE

1. Solid technique and strategy
2. Poise and maturity
3. Alert and relaxed nature
4. Unselfishness
5. Resilience
6. Focus and creativity
7. Consistency
8. Clear communication
9. Good eye contact
10. No blaming or excuse-making
11. Adaptability
12. Wise food choices
13. Intelligence and spatial awareness
14. Flexibility
15. Confidence
16. Imperturbable demeanor
17. Good reflexes and agility
18. Patience
19. Compassion
20. Team player

ABOUT THE AUTHOR

NICK GANCITANO was an All-American Soccer Player and Penn State Nittany Lion place-kicker when the team won the National Championship in 1983.

Nick received his degree in Exercise Sport Science (Biomechanics) and played briefly with the NFL's Detroit Lions. A knee injury retired him to the business world, where he became a regional vice-president for A.L. Williams. He later entered the public school system to teach science, coach wrestling, soccer and football, and train place-kickers. Since then, he has privately consulted dozens of place-kickers who received Division I college scholarships, some who went on to play professional football.

Nick's coaching, mentoring and consulting work has expanded to include athletes of all kinds. His emphasis on yoga, imagery, meditation and Self-inquiry has been instrumental in effectively bringing athletes into *The Zone*.

He currently lectures publicly and consults privately with athletes, teams, schools and businesses around the world. For seminar booking and consultations, visit www.NickGancitano.com.

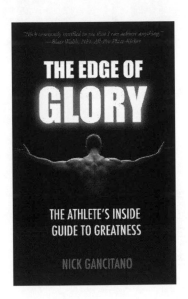

To Purchase Additional Copies of
The Edge of Glory:

www.NickGancitano.com

[Ebook Edition Also Available]

36628891R00149

Made in the USA
Charleston, SC
08 December 2014